RACHEL CROTHERS

Photo courtesy of The Billy Rose Theater Collection, The New York Public Library for the Performing Arts, Astor, Lenox and Tilden Foundations. Reprinted with permission.

RACHEL CROTHERS

A Research and Production Sourcebook

Colette Lindroth
and James Lindroth

Modern Dramatists Research and Production Sourcebooks, Number 8
William W. Demastes, Series Adviser

GREENWOOD PRESS
Westport, Connecticut • London

Library of Congress Cataloging-in-Publication Data

Lindroth, Colette.
    Rachel Crothers : a research and production sourcebook / Colette
Lindroth and James Lindroth.
        p.   cm.—(Modern dramatists research and production
sourcebooks, ISSN 1055-999X ; no. 8)
    Includes bibliographical references and indexes.
    ISBN 0-313-27815-6 (alk. paper)
    1. Crothers, Rachel, 1878-1958—Criticism and interpretation.
2. Women and literature—United States—History—20th century.
3. Crothers, Rachel, 1878-1958—Bibliography.   I. Lindroth, James
R.   II. Title.   III. Series.
PS3505.R895Z76   1995
812'.52—dc20   94-41267

British Library Cataloguing in Publication Data is available.

Library of Congress Catalog Card Number: 94-41267
ISBN: 0-313-27815-6
ISSN: 1055-999X

First published in 1995

Greenwood Press, 88 Post Road West, Westport, CT 06881
An imprint of Greenwood Publishing Group, Inc.

Printed in the United States of America

The paper used in this book complies with the
Permanent Paper Standard issued by the National
Information Standards Organization (Z39.48-1984).

10 9 8 7 6 5 4 3 2 1

Contents

Preface

This volume, *Rachel Crothers: A Research and Production Sourcebook*, is part of a series being published by Greenwood Press. The series will present extensive bibliographies, biographical essays, play synopses, production information and critical overviews of twentieth century dramatists. Books in the series are intended to serve both as quick reference guides and as exhaustive sources of production information.

This volume will make Crothers and her work accessible both to the scholar familiar with her career and to the student just discovering her. The biographical essay presents the significant details of Crothers's life and career along with a general picture of her critical reputation both now and during her lifetime, and suggestions of directions which future Crothers criticism might take. Following the biographical information each of Crothers's plays is summarized and a detailed account of its critical reception is provided, along with its stage history. While Crothers is primarily known for her plays she also worked for a time in Hollywood, and many of her plays were filmed, some more than once. Thus her film career is also considered in this section of the book.

An exhaustive bibliography of Crothers's own writing, both dramatic and journalistic, follows the summary section. Information on library collections of her manuscripts and other documents is also provided. The secondary bibliography, fully annotated and in chronological order, provides both factual information on individual reviewers' judgments of her work and a comprehensive overall picture of Crothers's reputation over nearly a century. As well as providing specific information the bibliographies can be "read" as a document in their own right, providing a vivid picture of Crothers's contribution both to the world of Broadway and to the larger world of social and political issues in the first half of the 20th century.

To make the sourcebook simple to use, bibliography entries and production information are coded according to their type. These codes, along with the indexes, make it easy to find all the relevant information for any play.

Acknowledgments

We would like to thank the staffs of several libraries for their courteous, efficient and knowledgeable assistance. In particular the staff members of the Billy Rose Collection in the Theater Collection of the New York Public Library have earned our gratitude for their unfailing courtesy, expertise and professionalism, as have the librarians at Caldwell College and the Milner Library of Illinois State University at Normal, Illinois. All these people were of great help in securing the varied materials used in this research. Finally, we must thank Sister Brigid Brady, O.P., whose knowledge of the mysteries of fourteenth century English poetry is rivaled only by her knowledge of the mysteries of twentieth century computers, and without whose assistance this manuscript could not have appeared.

A Note on Codes and Numbering

"A"--A prefix indicating newspaper and magazine articles by Crothers, listed in the Primary Bibliography.

"B"--A prefix indicating articles in reference works and other full-length studies. These references are listed in the Secondary Bibliography.

"I"--A prefix indicating newspaper or magazine interviews of Crothers. These are listed in the Secondary Bibliography.

"P"--A prefix indicating productions of plays listed in Productions and Credits.

"R"--A prefix indicating reviews and other articles. These articles are listed chronologically in the Secondary Bibliography.

Chronology

1878	Rachel Crothers is born 12 December in Bloomington, Illinois, the youngest of nine children of Dr. Eli K. Crothers and Marie DePew Crothers.
1891	Graduates from Illinois State Normal University High School in Normal, Illinois.
1892	Graduates after a year at the New England School of Dramatic Instruction.
1897	Goes to New York and becomes involved with the Stanhope-Wheatcroft School of Acting as student and teacher.
1899	Presentation of three one-act plays at the Madison Square Theatre is her introduction to the New York stage as dramatist.
1906	Professional debut as dramatist with *The Three of Us*, a Broadway hit.
1907	Supervises the London production of *The Three of Us*, with Ethel Barrymore starring.
1917	Founds and leads the Stage Women's War Relief.
1928	Is the only woman among five dramatists chosen to lecture at the University of Pennsylvania.
1930	Goes to Paris to direct French translation of *Mary the Third*.

1930   Is named by journalist Ida Tarbell as one of 50 Foremost Women in the United States.

1932   Founds and leads the Stage Relief Fund.

1933   Theatre Club declares *When Ladies Meet* outstanding play of 1933.

1934   Leaves for Hollywood and a contract with Metro-Goldwyn-Mayer.

1935   After an unsuccessful experience with M-G-M, Crothers signs an independent contract with Goldwyn to oversee the production of her own film, "Splendor." This ends her relationship with Hollywood.

1937   *Susan and God*, her last Broadway production, opens.

1938   *Susan and God* becomes the first original-cast Broadway production to be televised.

1938   Theatre Club names *Susan and God* outstanding play of 1938.

1939   Is awarded the Chi Omega National Achievement award for 1938 in a ceremony at the White House.

1940   Founds and leads the American Theater Wing Allied Relief Fund.

1958   Dies 6 July, at the age of 80.

RACHEL CROTHERS

Life and Career

Rachel Crothers was born 12 December 1878 in Bloomington, Illinois, the youngest of nine children in a family distinguished by intellectual achievement and untraditional career choices. Her grandfather, Elijah DePew, was a friend of Abraham Lincoln, and both her parents, Marie DePew Crothers and Eli K. Crothers, were physicians, her mother having taken up the study of medicine when she was 40. While there are suggestions that the family circle was not always as close as the nineteenth century ideal would have it--6-year-old Rachel apparently lived with an aunt in Massachusetts while her mother pursued her medical studies--there was never any doubt that achievements were expected of all the family members.

From the beginning Rachel was drawn to artistic and creative endeavors; she had written two novels, which she enjoyed reading aloud to her friends, by the time she was 13. Her interest in the stage soon took precedence, however, and she was writing and staging one-act plays (which she called sketches to allay the suspicions of straitlaced churchmen) based on Biblical subjects before she was out of her teens. Her early dramatic work was done both for the Sunday School classes she taught and for the Bloomington Dramatic Club, providing her with the experience of both private and public audiences.

At 13 Crothers graduated from the Illinois State Normal University High School, where she had done a course of classical study and English literature. Among her favorite authors were Shakespeare, Byron and Tennyson, and when she was chosen as one of the speakers for her graduation she based her oration on Alexander Pope's line "The Proper Study of Mankind is Man."

Her early completion of high school was followed by a year at the New England School of Dramatic Instruction, where she studied with English actor Henry Addison Pitt. She graduated in 1892 and returned to Bloomington, leaving there at the age of 18 for New York City and her real commitment to the theater. In New York she enrolled at the Stanhope-Wheatcroft Dramatic School, where she spent one year as a student and four as a teacher and coach. She made full use of her varied talents here, writing and directing one-act plays which were performed by the students. Her first professional appearance as a playwright on a New York stage came with her production of "Criss-Cross," "Elizabeth" and "Mrs. John Hobbs" for Stanhope-Wheatcroft students on 20 April 1899, at the Madison Square Theatre. Following her association with Stanhope-Wheatcroft she appeared as an actress with several New York stock companies for three years.

Throughout her career she took an active interest in all aspects of the stage, concerned with writing, casting, directing and producing, and she always praised her apprentice years at Stanhope-Wheatcroft for providing valuable lessons in the significance of accurate detail, from the most effective language to the most effective lighting. While her interviews are occasionally contradictory on early details, some suggesting she initially intended to be an actress, others asserting that playwriting was always her primary interest, there is never any doubt that the practical life of the stage was her chief formative influence. She denied studying her craft from other playwrights, insisting that anyone with a good sense of structure, and the desire, could write successful dramas; the talent is inborn, not learned.

The years of apprenticeship paid off handsomely. Her first play, *The Three of Us*, produced in 1906 when she was not yet 30, was a smash hit heralded as presaging a new age of realistic drama which was both serious and entertaining. From this point on she never looked back, producing 24 plays, many of which were substantial hits, over the next 30 years, in addition to several one-act plays and a substantial number of interviews and articles on the dramatic arts. Deemed America's leading woman playwright by many critics, her career dominated the Broadway stage during the first half of the twentieth century.

From the first, her contribution was seen to be in the field of realistic modern drama, more often than not with a focus on a significant contemporary problem. From the first, too, and throughout her career, Crothers was aligned with the commercial aspects of the theatrical world rather than with the numerous experimental, avant-garde movements in both America and Europe (she once told an interviewer that "Gene" O'Neill, fine dramatist though he was, might have profited from greater attention to structural detail and polish). From the beginning to the end of her career her comments emphasize her respect for the intelligence and taste of an educated American audience, and, while she has often been labelled an intellectual conservative, as early as 1912 she was praising this modern audience, women especially, for demanding new and serious subjects in drama.

The realism of her settings, whether a true-to-life Nevada mining camp (*The Three of Us*) or an entirely convincing New York boardinghouse (*39 East*) was praised by the critics throughout her career. It is worth remembering that she began to write in an era which favored, at least for popular consumption, lightweight farce or romantic escapism; this makes her successful insistence on slice-of-life realism, without the grim determinism of the naturalists, the more significant in the light of her enduring popularity. From the beginning she presented real people in real lives, and for the most part she made the audience love them.

The early success of *The Three of Us* was followed, however, by two relative failures, *The Coming of Mrs. Patrick* and *Myself-Bettina*, neither of which won critical acclaim or audience popularity, though both were mildly praised for the originality and freshness of their vision. These unsuccessful efforts, however, were followed by two of the most significant and controversial plays of her early years, *A Man's World* in 1910 and *Ourselves* in 1913. Both of these plays were staged by Crothers herself, as were most of her productions from that time on. Both plays establish one of her most important thematic concerns: the unfairness of the double standard of morality as applied to men and women in the first part of the twentieth century. Both plays present women who, although entirely different as individuals, are alike in their refusal to accept the injustice of this traditional standard. Frances Ware and Molly each reject a man because he will neither see the unfairness of the double standard nor accept her for herself alone. While some of Crothers's later heroines compromise, surrendering some of their own self-sufficiency in order to avoid the loneliness of which the playwright always seemed aware, Frances and Molly resolutely strike out on their own rather than settle for second best. The fact that *Ourselves* also dealt candidly with the lives of young prostitutes in a bleak reform school underscores the seriousness of Crothers's vision in these early plays.

It was never Crothers's practice to remain fixed in one position as a dramatist for long, however, and the years 1914-18 saw some of her happiest and most sentimental comedies, a direct contrast to the somberness of *Ourselves* and the attack on convention in *A Man's World*. These early years also demonstrate her dramatic sophistication and the extent to which she was at ease in the Broadway world. Crothers early understood the need for any playwright, especially a woman, to establish connections with strong individuals in the theatre, and from the first she showed an ability to work well with powerful people, especially women. Maxine Elliott, for example, gave Crothers the opportunity to produce *Myself-Bettina*, in which Elliott starred. Having seen and liked *The Three of Us*, Elliott asked Crothers to write a play for her; the result was *Myself-Bettina*, which Crothers adapted for the successful actress. Crothers later said that Elliott's business ability provided her a model proving that women could shoulder the entire responsibility of a Broadway show. This was a model which Crothers was often to follow in her career.

Similarly, in *Young Wisdom* Crothers provided the first opportunity for Edith and Mabel Taliaferro, two popular young actresses, to star together, and in both *The Heart of Paddy Whack* and *Once Upon a Time* she provided a new career direction for Chauncey Olcott, the immensely popular Irish singer and romantic lead, a move which won both playwright and actor favorable critical comment. This early ability to provide a stage vehicle while retaining her own distinctive voice was never lost by Crothers, who wrote successfully for Tallulah Bankhead and Gertrude Lawrence, among others.

The impact which the young Crothers made on the theatrical world can also be seen in a long interview of 1916 in the *New York Times Magazine* (I085), in which she is quoted as stating firmly that directors, not authors, control the future of the stage in America. The interview, which emphasizes the uniqueness of her position as both author and director in a milieu with few women in either role, treats Crothers as a force to be reckoned with on Broadway, quoting her at length on the subject of the relationships between actor and director and seeking her opinion of contemporary experiments on the European stage. Crothers is firm in her conviction that the stage is inevitably progressive, a strong force in the molding of public opinion, taste and morality.

Another, perhaps less serious indication of Crothers's acceptance into the world of significant theatrical figures is her collaboration in a "pot-boiling experiment" undertaken in 1915 by the Society of American Dramatists and Composers, led by the distinguished playwright Augustus Thomas. This experiment, one of the endeavors which negative critics cite as an example of Crothers's conventionality, was an exercise in committee writing, with Thomas settling questions of plot, tone, focus and the like by popular vote of the dramatists involved. Originally done as part of a classroom exercise, the project won a horrified response from voices of the avant garde and amused condescension from more traditional critics. Not surprisingly, it was an experiment marked mainly by its publicity value rather than any lasting effect on the theater, popular or otherwise. The difficulty of pigeonholing Crothers in any ideological stance is underlined by her involvement in the experiment, however, since it came only a few years after Thomas had written his own play, *As a Man Thinks*, in protest against Crothers's observations on male/female social inequality in *A Man's World*. Clearly Crothers was developing, both as dramatist and as individual, as someone who thought for herself and avoided "camps" of either side.

By 1917, however, another of Crothers's enduring passions was making itself heard--her strong sense of obligation to help others. As World War I dragged toward its fourth year she became one of the people who tried to do something other than sympathize from the sidelines, becoming the moving spirit in founding the Stage Women's War Relief. As numerous articles from New York newspapers attest, this organization not only provided quantities of hospital supplies, clothing and other materials to both soldiers and civilians, it also made free stage shows available to servicemen in New York City and gave financial assistance to theatrical families whose principal wage-earners were away at war (R099). Crothers was able to interest none other than George M. Cohan in this project; with his partner Sam H. Harris, Cohan provided entertainment for the men in nearby mobilization camps. One, at Fort Meyers, N.J., featured prizefighter James J. Corbett and songwriter Irving Berlin. Crothers herself went to Washington to confer with the Secretary of War on the kinds of assistance to be provided by the organization.

The Stage Women's War Relief, another example of Crothers's directorial and executive ability, soon had branches in Boston, Chicago, Philadelphia, Detroit, Los Angeles and San Francisco. After the war Crothers turned back to a sustained dramatic investigation of contemporary issues, especially an exploration of the lives of women in the postwar world. In 1920 she finally succeeded in bringing *He and She*, one of her most unflinching examinations of women's lives, to the Broadway stage. The production history of *He and She*, discussed elsewhere in this book, illustrates society's reluctance to consider questions of modern woman's real freedom seriously on stage. It also illustrates Crothers's determination that it should do so, a determination culminating in her taking the role of Ann Herford in the Broadway production. The furor over

Ann's bleak choice at the end--rejecting artistic success because it would jeopardize her daughter's development--was even larger than that ignited by the equally strong feminism of *A Man's World*. It is a furor which has still not died down; *He and She* has been staged several times since 1971.

Crothers's ability to capitalize on contemporary problems is also seen in the strength of the response to *Nice People* (1921), the first of her "flapper plays" dealing with disaffected young people and the possibility of bridging modern rebellion and traditional values. *Nice People* inspired sermons and articles (R146, I153, R164) by experts who found that she had expressed exactly the thought of the times. Crothers's exploration of contemporary issues continued with *Everyday* (1921) and *Mary the Third* (1923), which examined the role of love and marriage for the modern woman. Several interviews of the early twenties quote Crothers extensively on the subject of modern mores and parent/daughter relationships (I153, I182).

Crothers's professional stature at this time led to her being included in a series of lectures by dramatists at the University of Pennsylvania in 1928. Crothers found herself, as she so often did, the only woman among the five dramatists chosen (one of the others invited was Eugene O'Neill). She was also chosen to oversee the $7 million construction of the American Women's Association clubhouse on West 57th Street in New York City. In 1930 she went to Paris to direct a French translation of *Mary the Third*, and later that year she was chosen one of the "Fifty Foremost Women of the United States" by Los Angeles journalist Ida Tarbell (R210), a list including Gertrude Vanderbilt, Willa Cather, Edith Wharton and Edna St. Vincent Millay.

While Crothers's career was primarily marked by both professional and financial success, there were a few ill-fated ventures in the late twenties. Her backing of plays by other women writers, for example, was not destined for success; the debts incurred with Zoe Akins's *Thou Desperate Pilot* forced Crothers to mortgage her Connecticut home in order to repay them. This financial instability was not long-lasting, however, as royalties from the hugely successful *Let Us Be Gay* enabled her to pay off the debts, including the mortgage.

By 1932 Crothers's social activities were again reasserting themselves. Her response to the Great Depression was to form the Stage Relief Fund in an effort to help theater people who were hard-hit by the Broadway slump following the Crash of 1929. Collecting clothes, arranging for employment, sometimes giving out money, the Fund had helped more than 2,500 people before it was a year old, and the final number of individuals who received a variety of aid was calculated at close to 6,000 people.

It is a mark of Crothers's stature at this point in her career that President and Mrs. Franklin Delano Roosevelt attended a performance of one of her plays, *When Ladies Meet*, when it appeared at the National Theatre in Washington, D.C. in 1933. Mrs. Roosevelt, who had already seen it in New York, had enjoyed the play so much she arranged a special performance for the presidential party.

In 1934 Crothers embarked on one of her few comparatively unsuccessful ventures in the dramatic world--she went to Hollywood. The move was accompanied by much fanfare in the press, since Crothers had long rejected the idea of screenwriting. As early as 1917 she had joked to an interviewer that her one experience as a filmwriter had turned out a product entirely unrecognizable to its author, causing her to vow never to work in film again. This longstanding suspicion of Hollywood's respect for the playwright, coupled with her undisputed claim to the title of foremost woman dramatist in America, created great interest in her signing with Metro-Goldwyn-Mayer. Columnist Louella Parsons speculated that she would do a picture for Miriam Hopkins or Norma Shearer, who had starred in the film version of *Let Us Be Gay*, and gushed that "all of feminine Hollywood" was marveling at Crothers's courage in signing for a share of the profits rather than a flat salary. In October the Los Angeles papers praised her business sense on different grounds, stating with awe that she was earning $6,000 a week, "topped only by [Louis B.] Mayer and Garbo" and predicting great success. Samuel Goldwyn himself expressed extravagant admiration for Crothers in other articles, praising her talent, professionalism and willingness to take risks, and leaving no doubt that those qualities would justify her salary. Her initial assignment was to be "No More Ladies," adapted from a play by A. E. Thomas and starring Robert Montgomery and Joan Crawford.

It was not to be a successful relationship, however. By May of 1935 Crothers was back in New York, commenting with wry irony on the series of adaptations, re- and re-re-adaptations which rendered her own work on "No More Ladies" unrecognizable, and which she was certain would leave even Thomas, the original author, baffled. Evidencing the strong-mindedness that was her characteristic from childhood on, Crothers finally insisted, "politely but firmly," that her name be removed from the screen credits. She later made arrangements to work independently for Goldwyn, however, praising him for his respect for good work and for authorial autonomy. Her contract stipulated that she be permitted to work independently on an unproduced play she had written fifteen years earlier, "The House of Lorrimore." In an interview she commented at length on her control over the project, stating optimistically that her own success might mean that other authors would have more control over future projects. The resulting film, "Splendor," starring Miriam Hopkins and Joel McCrea and featuring Billie Burke and David Niven in supportiong roles, is still occasionally to be seen on cable television.

If Crothers formed only an uneasy alliance with Hollywood, however, the same could not be said of her relationship with Broadway, and her career on the New York stage ended as it began, with a smash hit. Crothers's last play, *Susan and God*, starring Gertrude Lawrence, played for 288 performances and was revived in regional and summer stock theaters for nearly 20 years after it was written. *Susan and God* also made cultural and social history by becoming one of the first subjects of the infant television industry in 1938. It was only fitting that the individual who, as a woman in a man's world, had broken new ground in 1906 and continued to do so for thirty years, should have been one of the first artists to see her work used in this pioneer industry.

In April of 1939 she went to the White House, where Eleanor Roosevelt presented her with the Chi Omega National Achievement Award for 1938. It was only the second time that it had been presented to a woman of the theater (the first to receive it was Katharine Cornell, in 1936). In his speech of presentation, Broadway critic John Mason Brown (R258) paid special attention to the uniqueness of Crothers's achievement as a woman in a field so entirely dominated by men. He also praised the durability of her career, commending her for staying abreast of changing times and capturing the look and sound of life in the first half of the twentieth century in America. She was also named writer of the most outstanding play of 1938 by the Theatre Club for *Susan and God*, having won the same award in 1933 for *When Ladies Meet.*

As she had before, however, and more completely this time, Crothers turned her attention from the stage to social needs in 1940. A year after World War II began in Europe and a year before America was involved, she founded the American Theater Wing Allied Relief Fund and became its president. She chose five other women of theatrical renown to begin the organization with her: Josephine Hull, Antoinette Perry, Gertrude Lawrence, Theresa Hepburn and Vera Allen (I264). As the enormous scrapbooks of clippings of this organization's work amply attest, the Allied Relief Fund became her chief activity throughout the war years. Although she was quoted more than once as saying she hoped to begin another play she also remarked that such ambitions were dwarfed by the larger issues of a society at war. She even questioned in 1941 (I260) whether it "was important" that she write another play.

The Allied Relief Fund was tireless, sponsoring entertainment for soldiers (including the Stage Door Canteen) staging War Bond drives and collecting endlessly for relief of refugees. The organization itself and especially Crothers as its founder and president received numerous civic awards for their activities. In April 1941, for example, she was awarded the Clare M. Senie Award by the members of the Drama Study Club for her war relief work.

While she wrote more plays after the end of the war, they were never produced. Toward the end of her life she told an interviewer (B259), speaking of World War II and the Korean conflict, "War is no time for comedy," and in fact her comic voice, if not her social activities, had been stilled. She died in her home in Connecticut in 1958, at age 80.

The question of Crothers's contribution to American stage history has long been argued. During her lifetime she was repeatedly called the dean of women playwrights, or Broadway's most prominent woman playwright, but the condescending adjective "woman" was always used--the question of whether she was a truly major playwright, irrespective of her sex, hardly arose. Her commercial success was never questioned, but her very ability to please Broadway and international audiences over a thirty-year period has been used against her by critics who contend that this kind of crowd-pleasing precludes her being considered a serious artist. Even her status as a feminist has been argued; to many early critics she was too harsh, too pessimistic, too hard on men, while later critics saw her as betraying feminist principles for ticket-selling happy endings. Still other critics see her later plays as muddled or sentimental retreats from the staunch feminism of *The Three of Us* or *A Man's World*. Even her universally conceded ability to produce a perfectly structured play often means she is criticized for producing facile artifice instead of profound questions. And certainly her stature has dwindled; from being one of the most powerful women of the theater in the first half of the twentieth century she has become almost ignored today.

Somewhere between the extremes of adulation and rejection can be found the real value and contribution of Rachel Crothers. To begin with perhaps the simplest element: her significance as a pioneer woman in a man's field is unarguable. Even woman playwrights were a rare breed when she began writing, and the amount of control she exerted over all aspects of the production of her plays was entirely unprecedented. In "Troubles of a Playwright" (A09), "The Producing Playwright" (A06) and other articles, she paid tribute to the examples of women like Maxine Elliott and Mary Kirkpatrick who first showed that women had the business ability to produce Broadway shows. Certainly Crothers herself, with her long and financially successful career, also provides ample proof that women can succeed in the business of Broadway.

In assessing Crothers's social attitudes, especially her attitudes toward women, it is time to look at her work with an eye unprejudiced by the approaches of the past. It is easy to oversimplify her ideas by focusing, as many of her critics have done, on one obvious spokeswoman in each play. Thus one reads that Kitty's return to Bob in *Let Us Be Gay*, Lucile's return to Charles in *As Husbands Go*, the youngest Mary's callow pronouncements in *Mary the Third*, or even Gail and Victoria Claffenden's youthful nonsense in *Young Wisdom* conveys Crothers's "meaning." If that were the case, Crothers could indeed be found guilty of retrograde thinking on feminism. But Crothers's works demand that one listen to all the voices of the play, a chorus of differing, complex meanings rather than one simple one.

Excluding some of the works which Crothers herself said were unrelated to her "Comedy Humaine de la Femme," like *Once Upon a Time* or *Caught Wet*, the chorus of voices in a typical Crothers play reveals an honest picture of middle-class female life in years of drastic change for women. One frequent critical mistake has been to ignore or condescend to her frivolous, often selfish voices, like Emmie in *As Husbands Go* or Bridget in *When Ladies Meet*. Silly though Emmie and Bridget often are, they speak profound and painful truths about limitations. Alone, relegated by family members to old age while still in their vigorous forties, looking with wistful resentment at male sexual freedom, Emmie and Bridget demand their share of fun, of excitement, of life not lived in the shadow of a husband. They are also painfully realistic, speaking with dignity of the loneliness which was their lot even when they were married-- sometimes worse than when they are widowed. Dismissing characters like these as convenient dramatic foils created by a playwright bent on the artificiality of the "well-made play" misses the point that middle-aged women often are wounded by daughters who dismiss them as sexual beings, that widows often are lonely, that women often do sacrifice their integrity for male companionship to combat that loneliness. Emmie and Bridget may not be heroic, strong-minded feminists, but they are realistic, and they speak as eloquently for superfluous, unappreciated women as Rhy or Frances Ware do for strong, independent ones. The lonely, desperate women of Crothers's plays--Clara (*A Man's World*),

Mamie (*Myself-Bettina*), Ellinor (*The Coming of Mrs. Patrick*), Margaret Flinn (*The Heart of Paddy Whack*), Daisy (*He and She*), Margaret Rainsford (*Nice People*), Mrs. Nolan (*Everyday*) and Irene, Charlotte and Leonora (*Susan and God*) speak to the limitations of women's lives as powerfully, although negatively, as Ann Herford or Ruth Creel (*He and She*) speak to their potential.

The effect of the voices heard together is more powerful than that of a single character. In *Everyday*, for example, at least four completely different attitudes are expressed. Phyllis is rebellious and idealistic, while May is superficial and vain. Mrs. Raymond is frankly exploitative and predatory, while Mrs. Nolan is almost obliterated by her husband's powerful personality. Individually any one of these characters might seem oversimplified; heard together, they offer a powerful statement on possibilities and limitations. The ending of the play might seem too convenient--Phyllis stands by her ideals and presumably wins her equally highly-principled man--but the problems of the other women are not solved at all, and they are real problems of real women. Certainly Crothers did write "audience-pleasing comedies." She also presents much that is less reassuring than her happy endings, however, for those who choose to widen the focus beyond one or two main chararacters.

Serious attention to the varied chorus of voices also exonerates Crothers from the criticism that too many of her characters are meant to provide only smart, witty dialogue, empty of real meaning and catering to a fashionable, superficial audience. She was a master of witty repartee, but it is rarely if ever empty of meaning. The badinage of the sophisticated young things of *A Little Journey* or *Nice People*, for example, still creates a vivid portrait of bored, disaffected postwar youth, as powerful an evocation of the early twenties as anything in F. Scott Fitzgerald. The conversation of the younger generation in *Mary the Third, As Husbands Go* or even as slight an effort as *Caught Wet* reveals an underlying sense of disillusionment and bitterness which is far from being simply entertaining. Crothers's witty repartee was meant to, and did, please a large audience; it also tells the modern reader a great deal about human attitudes and emotions in the early twentieth century. Beyond that, it is well worth reading for its own sake. Crothers was as adept at colloquial language as any American dramatist has ever been. Her slang, especially, is as fresh and undated now as it was in 1906, 1921 or 1937, and her fresh, vivid language presents a memorable portrait of the nature of the lives she portrays.

It is also a critical oversimplification to conclude that most of her plays show women who happily accept traditional roles. Many of her heroines do end up accepting love and domesticity--Rhy MacChesney, Kitty Brown, Lucile Lingard, Susan Trexel, for example. Others, however, do not: Frances Ware, Molly, Mary Howard. And even for those who do there are strong suggestions that the "happy ending" is sometimes only a temporary solution. When Kitty embraces Bob at the end of *Let Us Be Gay* she is as much in retreat from loneliness and frustration as she is in love with him, and the philandering which caused her to leave him is still a part of his character, however prudent he might be at the moment. Similarly, when Susan embraces Barrie at the end of *Susan and God* the problems which drove them apart, especially his drinking, have not magically disappeared. Kitty, Susan and other Crothers heroines are faulty, limited women who accept faulty, limited men rather than consign themselves to loneliness. In this they only superficially fit the requirements for the happy ending; the reader who wonders what happens after the curtain falls will realize that this is the literature of emotional realism rather than of saccharine happy endings. When Crothers intends to create a fairy tale effect, as she does in *Once Upon a Time*, she makes it quite clear that a dramatist's magic wand is meant to guarantee a "happily ever after" ending. When she does not, she suggests the painful reality of real lives. While her comments throughout her life attest to her belief in the healing power of love, her plays demonstrate that she knew that healing power had only limited, not magical properties.

Crothers's plays, then, are well worth serious study for their intrinsic worth, as documents revealing evolving social attitudes in the first half of the twentieth century in language as fresh and vivid as it was when it was written. Even better, if possible, would be to read Crothers accompanied by her critics. The combination of her complex vision, her popular acceptance by audiences, and the comments of her critics, both favorable and unfavorable, presents an incomparable history of changing attitudes toward women in the first half of the twentieth century.

The Plays and Films: Summaries and Critical Overviews

The following is a collection of summaries and critical overviews of Crothers's plays and of the one film over which she exerted significant artistic control. Filmed versions of several of her plays, in which she was not artistically involved, are also mentioned. Each critical overview includes a brief description of the play's stage history including significant revivals and touring productions. The nature of the critical reception is given in each case, as well as mention of significant wider social response when Crothers was dealing with such controversial issues as female independence, the condition of marriage as an institution, and issues of young people's morality in the 1920's. Specific references to many reviews provide a clear picture of Crothers's stature in the world of Broadway from 1906 through World War II.

When specific reviews and articles are referred to in this section, parenthetical citations refer to the code number of the source as it is listed in the Secondary Bibliography section of this book.

The Three of Us (1906)

The Characters: RHY MAC CHESNEY: An orphan, a strong-willed young woman faced with the challenge of being both head of a family and a successful miner when everyone around her tells her she will fail; CLEM MAC CHESNEY: her younger brother, resentful at their difficult and unrewarding life and anxious to find a more glamorous existence; "SONNIE" MAC CHESNEY: their 13-year-old brother, very much "all boy"; LOUIS BERRESFORD: a rich young man in love with Rhy; STEPHEN TOWNLEY: a poor young man in love with Rhy; MRS. TWEED BIX: a strong-minded, mature woman who intends to sell her successful mine and move back to New York; TWEED BIX: her English husband; LORIMER TRENHOLM: the wealthy man who intends to buy the Bixes' mine; MAGGIE: the MacChesneys' devoted servant; HOP WING: Berresford's manservant.

Plot Summary--ACT I: The scene is "the present" on a winter morning in a

Nevada mining camp, in the MacChesney living room, roughly furnished with old-fashioned, well-worn furniture. Conversation at the breakfast table among Maggie, Sonnie, Clem and Rhy establishes the MacChesneys as a close-knit family, hard-working and self-sufficient, led by the independent Rhy. Their parents have been dead for eight years. There are problems looming, however; Clem is becoming discontented, wanting to strike out on his own, and their mine (its name, "The Three of Us," tells the audience how much their dead father wanted them to stay together) is not productive. Added to this is the fact that both Louis Berresford and Steve Townley are in love with Rhy, who would rather succeed at the mine than marry anyone just now.

Towards the end of the first act Townley tells Rhy, in strictest confidence, that he's staked a claim on a mine that was considered played-out but is still productive. He has a scheme--an honest one--to get Trenholm to buy the Bix mine, which shares the vein with his, at a better price than he might otherwise pay. Trenholm will get a share of Townley's mine in return for financing him.

Rhy thinks she hears something but decides it's her imagination. Townley and Rhy romance a bit, then exit separately. Enter Clem, surreptitiously; when Berresford enters looking for Rhy, Clem clearly implies his intention to betray Townley's overheard confidence in return for enough money to enable him to take off on his own.

ACT II: In Mrs. Bix's living room, which, like the MacChesney home, reflects good taste, an artistic sensibility and not much money. Mrs. Bix and Rhy are both dressed elegantly if quaintly.

Amid much jovial party-talk, it becomes clear that Townley is as straightforward and honest as Berresford is sneaky and dishonest. Berresford tricks Rhy; she has said that "keeping secrets is her long suit," and suddenly he tells her--in confidence--that he has bought the Bix mine earlier that morning. When Trenholm makes Mrs. Bix an offer, she is taken aback (clearly Berresford had implied Trenholm was no longer interested) but says that, having sold her mine, she has no further say in the matter.

Trenholm is understandably angry because he thinks people are trying to inflate land prices behind his back; Townley is understandably angry because he assumes that Rhy betrayed his confidence. Rhy says nothing because she feels bound to respect Berresford's confidence. The act ends with Townley furiously accusing Rhy of having made a fool of him.

ACT III: The scene is Berresford's living room, a sort of hunting lodge. Conversation between Berresford and Hop Wing reveals Berresford as authoritarian and disagreeable.

Suddenly Rhy enters, much to Berresford's amazement. He recovers quickly, however, and offers a drink which she refuses firmly. She asks to be released from her promise of confidence; he refuses. As they argue it becomes clear that he has done everything to compromise her. Anything she does will look bad, including--perhaps most of all--her coming to his home so late at night. He is clearly, and intentionally, taking advantage of her, a fact she begins to realize. (As they talk she discovers Clem's watch-fob and seal on the floor and begins to realize, with fury, what has been happening.)

Berresford is ardent and romantic, eager to protect her from the predicament he contrived for her; she rejects him, confessing she loves Townley, which makes Berresford even more disagreeable. He promises her his love and "everything that money can give" her, but when asked if he is proposing, he equivocates, saying only that marriage "will come," apparently later. She realizes her predicament, especially the potential for scandal in her appearing at his place so late. She is, however, willing to bet that Townley, since he loves her, will believe only the best of her.

Townley appears, and is only too willing to believe the worst of everyone. The men fight, and everyone but Rhy insists that the only way to save her good name is by marrying Berresford. She defends her honor and her independence: "Don't you dare to speak of my honor and my good name! My honor! Do you think it's in your hands? It's in my own and I'll take care of it, and of everyone who *belongs* to me. I don't need you--either of you." She rushes from the room.

ACT IV: The MacChesney living room again. Rhy is in despair, but as she and Clem argue she realizes that he needs more freedom. He in turn realizes that he has done a dishonorable thing. He leaves to return the $500 Berresford had given him.   Townley comes in; Rhy passionately tells him she did *not* tell Berresford about the mine, but still cannot tell him who did--she has given her word. She loves him too much to care about details; she tells him she would marry him any time he asked, and vows that she has "never been anything but true" to him. Finally he is convinced by her eloquence and her obvious sincerity.

There is still the matter of Rhy's scandalous presence in Berresford's room late at night, however. Clem, and even Mrs. Bix, are shocked by her rash behavior, but Rhy simply doesn't care about appearances, and finally the others are won over to her way of thinking. Townley begins to realizes that Berresford had trapped Rhy because of her own honesty and sense of honor, and he dismisses the deceptive appearance of the scene he had stumbled into the night before. The play ends with "the three of us"--Rhy, Clem and Sonnie--still together, joined by the protective and loving Townley.

Critical Overview--*The Three of Us*, Crothers's first Broadway production and her first smash hit, opened at the Madison Square Theater (NY) on 17 October 1906 to almost universal critical praise. Produced by Walter N. Lawrence and staged by George Foster Platt, it played 227 performances (P1.1). Critics hailed its honesty, its natural realism and moral tone, predicting nothing but success for this new playwright. After its initial Broadway success it toured extensively, and in 1907 a London production, overseen by Crothers, opened with Ethel Barrymore in the lead role.

The reviewer for the *New York World* (R001) praised Crothers, "a mere novice at playwriting," for her "authentic and sympathetic picture of life," her "photographic reality" and her dramatic, fresh, original voice. He praised the entire cast, especially Carlotta Nillson as Rhy. Alan Dale in the *New York American* (R003) was enthusiastic about the fresh, vigorous human appeal in the play, finding the acting "exquisitely modulated" and the play's effect "flawless." Rhy's characterization was pronounced especially impressive, the hallmark of the true dramatist.

The *Blue Book* reviewer (R011) was especially pleased by the Americanness of the play, which could present all the realism of a mining camp without becoming sordid or depressing. Like the others, this review was especially impressed by the characterization of Rhy, the "stout-hearted, loyal sister" who embodies all the family values. *The Theatre Magazine* (R014), while finding that the play was too loosely constructed, concluded that it "wins on its simplicity and genuineness," adding that there is great promise for the future of this playwright who has "eyes of love for human nature."

Most of the reviews for the touring productions were also enthusiastic. The *Kansas City Post* (R012), while finding the characters a bit overdrawn, found universal appeal in the play's message and commended Crothers for avoiding the conventional ingredients, oversimplified characters and situations of melodrama. The *Louisville Herald* (R010) lavished extravagant praise, citing the play's "wealth of deep, true feeling," its "refreshing originality" and genuine power. The review also suggested that the play was more sophisticated than its audience, which had a deplorable tendency to laugh at inappropriate moments. The reviewer concluded that *The Three of Us* was "one of the finest, truest pieces of stage literature" to come to Louisville in years. The *St. Louis Star* (R013), however, was not so positive, finding the play heavy, tiresome and too long. The theme was dismissed as hackneyed and the tone as cloying and sweet.

The reviewer for the *Chicago News* (R005) found the play the "sweetest, truest, most brilliantly dramatic literary event of the season," praising its "simple poetry," its "superb ethics," its charm and conciseness. The review praised Crothers for avoiding melodramatic conventions, especially those associated with Western dramas. The *Toledo Blade* (R008) was equally positive, finding in the play a virility beyond that expected in the writing of a woman dramatist. The review praised Crothers for her ability to write strong scenes and big characters without sacrificing the gentle touches and fine feelings, the "many little glints of light and shade which only a woman can give."

The Coming of Mrs. Patrick (1907)

The Characters--MR. LAWTON: The worn, weary head of a family, a man whose wife has been ill for three years; BILLY LAWTON: 21, his rebellious son; NINA LAWTON: 19, overcome by her inability to help her mother or the rest of the family; ELLINOR LAWTON: 25, running the family but weighed down by its burdens; TOM CROWELL and DUDLEY BIRMINGHAM; in love with Nina; DR. BRUCE: 40, vigorous and handsome; Ellinor is unconsciously in love with him; MRS. PATRICK: the nurse who comes to care for Mrs. Lawton and in so doing changes the family's lives; CHRISSY HEATH: in love with Billy; PAULINE SHANK: a friend of Billy and Nina; MATTHEWS and MARIA: servants.

Plot Summary--ACT I: Evening at the Lawton house, cold, gloomy and forbidding. Mrs. Lawton has been gravely ill for three years, and the strain is beginning to tell on the family. Ellinor has assumed the entire burden of caring for her mother and running the family, but her rigid idealism and insistence on martyring herself are making both her and everyone around her unhappy. Billy has become sulky and rebellious, Nina helpless and childish. Mr. Lawton is nearly defeated. Dr. Bruce, who is treating the sick woman, realizes that changes must be made; he has arranged for a new nurse, Mrs. Patrick, to come to the house. Ellinor is resentful, feeling her authority questioned and her position usurped.

Immediately upon entrance Mrs. Patrick impresses the audience as an unusual woman, able to intuit the hidden strains and stresses of all the Lawtons. She immediately tries to lighten the mood, calling for Pauline to play the piano and arranging for Mrs. Lawton to be moved to another floor. Ellinor demands that the dancing and music be stopped, insisting that the noise will annoy the sick woman and refusing to let her be moved. She effectively cancels Mrs. Patrick's attempts to create a more relaxed and cheerful atmosphere.

ACT II: Six weeks later, at an evening dinner party attended by Birmingham, Crowell, Nina, Billy, Pauline, and Dr. Bruce and Ellinor. The hints that Mrs. Patrick knew some of these people earlier become confirmed when Birmingham pointedly asks her not to reveal their past relationship. She agrees, but, since she dislikes him, she arranges for Pauline to flirt with Crowell so that Nina will pay less attention to Birmingham and more to Crowell. Birmingham, realizing that Mrs. Patrick is hindering his chances with Nina, suggests to Ellinor that Mrs. Patrick is not to be trusted and that she is pursuing Dr. Bruce.

Romantic entanglements come thick and fast as Billy, who is drinking considerably too much, reveals his plan to elope at midnight with Chrissy Heath. Mrs. Patrick decides, after trying more reasonable tactics, to get him so drunk he won't be able to leave; to her surprise he declares his love of her, and proposes. Just then Dr. Bruce and Ellinor walk in on them. Mrs. Patrick refuses to defend herself in this compromising position, and so the worst suspicions appear to be confirmed. Mrs. Patrick will leave the Lawton home.

ACT III: The next morning; Mrs. Patrick is preparing to leave. Nina tells her she is going to marry Birmingham; Mrs. Patrick understands her decision but begs her to wait before making a mistake she will regret forever. Mrs. Patrick also tries to convince Chrissy not to marry Billy, for the same reason; when Ellinor enters and insists that Mrs. Patrick give Billy up, Chrissy begins to realize that things are not what she had thought. The young people leave and Mrs. Patrick reveals that she had no intention of marrying a boy as young as Billy, but that she had been trying to prevent his imprudent elopement. Ellinor, realizing how wrong she has been, begs Mrs. Patrick's forgiveness; she and Dr. Bruce beg her to reconsider leaving, but she is adamant. A plea on the part of Mrs. Lawton, who needs her care so desperately, however, convinces her to stay.

ACT IV. Two months later; Mrs. Lawton is said to be recovering. The romantic entanglements are still somewhat in evidence as Birmingham tries to compromise Mrs. Patrick's credibility. Finally Mrs. Patrick reveals that Birmingham has had an earlier affair with Chrissy, thus revealing how utterly inappropriate both Birmingham and Chrissy are for Nina and Billy. Finally even Ellinor is convinced of Mrs. Patrick's goodness, her generosity, her desire to help others, to "give, give, give" unstintingly. As she speaks to Mrs. Patrick, Ellinor herself begins to change, suddenly becoming more gentle, more beautiful, more open to others. As Dr. Bruce observes this he can no longer restrain himself; he announces his love of Mrs. Patrick. She, however, will not have him until she is assured, by both of them, that the feeling between Bruce and Ellinor is only warm friendship. By the end of the play all is well romantically: Billy is paired with Pauline, Nina with Crowell, and Dr. Bruce with Mrs. Patrick. Even Ellinor is now free to pursue her own life. Fittingly, as the play ends the audience hears Mrs. Lawton, who has not been seen during the entire play, descending the stairs. Flowers are tossed on the steps to greet her return to health and the family.

Critical Overview--*The Coming of Mrs. Patrick* opened 6 November 1907 at the Madison Square Theater (NY) to mixed reviews. It played 13 performances (P2.1). While critics found it generally pleasant, nearly everyone contrasted its ineffective structure to the skill evident in *The Three of Us*.

The *New York Evening Post* (R017), for example, praised the picture of Mrs. Patrick, enjoying the idea of "a brave, generous and loving woman who devotes herself to the well-being of others, endures tribulation...and at last finds happiness." The play itself, however, was found to be "an exceedingly crude affair," slow and poorly structured. The *New York Telegram* (R021) found it "interesting in a feeble and feminine way," but pronounced it too slow-moving, declaring that the only members of the audience who were not hysterical with inappropriate laughter were bored and depressed. The acting of Laura Nelson Hall in the lead role, however, was praised.

The *New York Mirror* (R020) also found it too slow and talky, saying more action was needed. *The Theatre Magazine* (R019) praised the play as being part of a movement away from conventionality and towards "newness of subject and character," finding this a healthy departure from stock characters and situations. The play lacked some balance and had "remnants of artificiality," but its merits outweighed its flaws. The *New York Times* (R018), however, flatly disagreed, declaring that "if departure from theatrical conventions means many more plays like this," it would be better to go back to "any old school, where each step has some bearing on what follows next." The play was dismissed as being "no end of talk and artificial incident, with action that is so very natural that it is almost always trivial." The reviewer added that Crothers's reputation, which had established itself so successfully with her first effort, *The Three of Us*, was not enhanced by this work.

Myself-Bettina (1908)

The Characters--JOHN MARSHALL: an intense, dedicated, rather straitlaced young minister in a New England town; LENNOX MARSHALL: his younger brother; CHRISTINE MARSHALL: his older sister and housekeeper, at 45 a humorless, censorious woman; BETTINA DEAN: a beautiful, vibrant, willful young woman just returned to her New England home town after studying voice in Europe; MAMIE DEAN: her younger half-sister; ANNABELLE GREENLEAF: a neighbor; CHARLES HOPE: an impressionable young neighbor; ABBIE: the Marshalls' servant; BEN: a neighbor boy.

Plot Summary--ACT I. The setting is a gracious, lovely, century-old Colonial house, the Marshall residence. Christine and Abbie are cleaning and discussing the imminent arrival of Bettina, their young neighbor. Their gossip reveals a local scandal: Bettina's mother, at her death, had left more money to her own daughter, Bettina, than to her step-daughter, Mamie. Bettina's use of her inheritance to go to Paris to study singing did not quiet the gossip. When the scene changes the audience discovers that Mamie and Lennox are in love but cannot afford to marry yet, and that there is some dark, hidden problem; Mamie says, of this secret, "If [Bettina] should ever find out I'd die," and Lennox consoles her.

Bettina enters in a whirl of talk and excitement, happy to be home but enthusiastically singing the praises of Parisian culture and sophistication, and criticizing the naive provinciality of New England in comparison. She challenges John, who is obviously fascinated by her, to "*do* something" instead of wasting himself in a small town. She intends to become an opera singer and is not interested in John's praise of Mamie's voice, heard in the church choir, especially when John hints it might be better than Bettina's. John disapproves of her frivolity, especially when she sings a "clever but naughty French song"; Lennox, on the other hand, is intrigued.

ACT II. Two months later. Everyone is busily arranging an elaborate party, but all is not well; Mamie clearly resents Lennox's fascination with Bettina. Bettina boasts of how moral she has become for New England; she hasn't "smoked a cigarette or danced a step" in two months. John is generally upset and disapproving; Bettina seems to enjoy shocking and upsetting him. John continues to hint that she should sacrifice some of her good fortune to help Mamie.

More conversation reveals that the local drama club is producing "Salome," and that Bettina will sing--and dance--the lead role. Christine and John are horrified; when Charles weakly tries to defend it as a "Biblical subject" no one is fooled. Everyone ends up quarreling over something--Mamie and John jealous of Lennox's attention to Bettina, and Bettina herself rather put off by the speedy development of his attentions. As the act ends she challenges John: "When I left you were a man--when I came back you were only a preacher," and asks him to give up his convictions for her love. When he refuses she stalks off.

ACT III. Two days later, 5 a.m. Mamie enters the room stealthily, then hides; she is followed by Lennox and Bettina, both in evening dress. When Lennox professes his love for Bettina she pushes him away; Mamie reveals herself and a three-way argument ensues. Finally Bettina asks Mamie, "Do you mean--you're *not* married--and you *ought* to be?" Mamie bursts into tears as Bettina reproaches her for the disgrace this brings to the family, then complains that Bettina, who been so lucky, has no right to criticize her. Christine enters and

Mamie hides; Christine insists that Bettina must marry Lennox because they were out all night together. Bettina refuses, and when Christine protests she bursts out "I will not be dictated to!" She continues to protest at the stifling atmosphere in this New England village, unaware that John has entered. John, who has heard her outburst, again compares her unfavorably to the well-behaved Mamie, at which point Mamie's sobs betray her presence, and she confesses to John "I should have married Lennox--a long time ago."

John is horrified and Bettina turns her criticism on him, blaming his New England rigidity for Mamie's rebellion. There is a lengthy discussion of real goodness, conformity and morality, and John begins to relent; he confesses that he has been too harshly judgmental. At this Bettina too softens, blaming herself for deserting Mamie and going off to indulge herself in Paris. She decides to send Mamie to Paris to study instead of returning herself. When John says this would create a "good excuse to hurry" their marriage, Bettina won't hear of it: no matter what Mamie's condition, she and Lennox must not marry without real love. Finally John agrees, reluctantly. The play ends with the decision that Mamie will not marry, but instead go to Paris to "begin again." Bettina and John reveal their love to each other as the play ends.

Critical Overview--*Myself-Bettina* opened 5 October 1908 at Daly's Theatre (NY). It played 32 performances, having toured extensively before its New York opening (P3.1).

The critics, while praising Maxine Elliott's audience appeal and beauty, were not kind to her or the play. The *New York Sun* (R029) found it disappointing, trite, imitative and insincere; the *New York Tribune* (R024), criticizing its "vulgar heralding of an alleged 'Salome' dance," accused Crothers of exhibiting "the frailties of her sex" in the play and called it one of the poorest presentations of the season. Charles Darnton in the *New York Evening World* (R022) was especially critical of the play's emphasis on sexuality: "It had to come, this Salome business...but it was hardly expected that it would fall flat with such a thud as it did last night." Darnton also attacked Elliott, stating that although "she had surrounded herself with the plainest women seen on a Broadway stage since 'Mrs. Wiggs of the Cabbage Patch,'" it was "utterly impossible for her to shine even by contrast with her deadly surroundings." He pronounced it "the season's most utter failure." The *Times* (R023) was a bit kinder, finding the play interesting but questioning the timing, since Crothers's ideas had been developed recently, and better, in other plays.

The Theatre Magazine (R027) complained about "faulty technical management" which obscured the play's points, concluding that it "missed its mark," while *Blue Book Magazine* (R026) simply wondered "what Miss Crothers is doing with her talent."

Critical reaction was so severe that an article in the *Toledo Blade* (R028) reviewing recent New York openings criticized the critics for their violent attack on *Myself-Bettina* and its star. Even the *Blade*, however, complained that Crothers "must needs preach a sermon, teach a lesson, draw a moral," and that she insisted on "a discussion of sex problems that are best left undiscussed before a mixed audience." The reviewer concluded that Crothers's intentions were good enough, but that her execution, in this play at least, was faulty.

Elsewhere in the tour, reviewers in Baltimore, Philadelphia and Chicago praised Elliott's appeal to her audience, but they too complained about the didacticism and sentimentality of the play. The *Philadelphia Inquirer* (R025) somewhat grudgingly conceded that the play would "probably please women," but only because it was full of "the same pleasing homely details that largely atoned for an unconsequential story" in Crothers's first play.

A Man's World (1910)

The Characters--(All characters live at the boardinghouse which is the play's setting) FRANCES "FRANK" WARE: a successful novelist, a woman who is "strong, free, unafraid, with the glowing charm of a woman at the height of her development"; CLARA OAKES: a mousey spinster, an artist who works in miniatures and is timidly arranging for a small show in the boardinghouse; FRITZ BAHN, EMILE GRIMEAUX and WELLS TREVOR: fellow boarders all more or less in love with Frank, and all type characters--Fritz straightforwardly Germanic, Emile a Frenchman more than a little amused by puritanical American attitudes, Wells the young American go-getter; LEONIE BRUNE: an aspiring actress, jealous of Frank and therefore quick to disapprove of her behavior; MALCOLM GASKELL: a successful, ambitious businessman, in love with and loved by Frank; KIDDIE: a 7-year-old orphan adopted by Frank; while he is not her child the scandalous possibility that he might be fascinates all who know them.

Plot Summary--ACT I: Evening in a shabby but comfortable rooming house filled with amusing Bohemian types. Kiddie waits impatiently for Frank's return while Fritz, Emile, Leonie and Clara discuss her work and their career ambitions. When Frank enters we discover that Frank had adopted Kiddie while she was in Paris working on a book; his mother, an unnamed American girl, died giving birth and Frank took the infant only because no one else would. Now, however, she loves him devotedly. The "gang" at the boardinghouse is somewhat disapproving, however; they point out that her position as a single mother invites scandal, and it is clear that at least a few people, including Leonie, suspect that he is in fact her son. Frank treats the threat of scandal with contempt and brushes off suggestions that she proceed more cautiously.

When Gaskell enters it is clear that he and Frank are strongly attracted, but that his domineering tendencies will cause trouble with such an independent woman. He praises her new book but complains that her female protagonist "rail[s] against men and the world." He affirms with amused condescension that "Man sets the standard for woman," demanding that she be better than he is, and that this is how things will always be: "Women are only meant to be loved--and men have got to take care of them." Frank argues and the act ends with them quarreling, but still obviously in love.

ACT II. Clara and Leonie's room. Clara, Fritz and Leonie are speculating on the identity of Kiddie's father. As Clara sets up her art show Leonie points out that Kiddie's miniature bears a startling resemblance to Gaskell. Over Leonie's protests, the picture is removed from the show. When Fritz tries to warn Frank that the gossip is getting dangerous she becomes impatient and angry; she is even more upset later when Gaskell also presses her on the subject of Kiddie, asking her to give him up because of the danger of scandal. Challenging him, she asks him if he would refuse to marry her if Kiddie were indeed her child; he refuses a direct answer. After he leaves Frank looks at Kiddie's picture and realizes why Fritz and the others were upset: "They mean that Kiddie looks like me," she says as the curtain falls.

ACT III: Frank is listening to Kiddie read; significantly, he is having trouble with the word "f-a-t-h-e-r." Frank and Gaskell quarrel, more seriously this time; they patch it up again, however. When Clara, discouraged by the failure of her attempt at an art show, enters, she defines the plight of the unprotected woman: "I've tried just as hard as I can for ten years...and look at me--I don't even know how I am going to pay my next month's rent. I'm so sick and tired of it all I don't know what to do. I'd marry any man that asked me." She goes on: "I've always been superfluous and plain...I'm just one of those everlasting women the world is full of. There's nobody to take care of me and I'm simply not capable of taking care of myself." Frank encourages her, asking her to help by teaching drawing at a girls club that she is starting. Clara, thrilled to be needed by someone, agrees.

When Fritz and Leonie enter, Leonie reveals that she thinks Kiddie resembles Gaskell, not Frank; Frank is horrified, but obviously beginning to realize that he does. She insists that she truly doesn't know who the father is, but has "hated him all these years," because he deserted "Kiddie's poor little mother" and the baby. Leonie responds, "Men are pigs of course. They take all they can get and don't give any more than they have to. It's a man's world--that's the size of it."

Enter Kiddie and Gaskell, who are getting on famously. Gaskell thinks Frank should reveal the identity of Kiddie's mother, to save her own reputation; she refuses. As she looks at him, she realizes that Leonie was right about the resemblance. When she asks if he ever knew a girl named Alice Ellery he is startled and defensive: "Who told you that?" Frank understands everything now. She rejects him, after telling him that Kiddie really *is* his child.

ACT IV: Kiddie wonderingly asks what's wrong; Frank tries to reassure him. Gaskell tries to convince her that she still loves him, that he has committed no serious wrong; she is unforgiving. When he insists that women must forgive men she speaks up for the people he wronged: "If he hadn't been put into my arms a little helpless, nameless thing--if I hadn't seen that girl suffer the tortures of hell through her disgrace, I probably wouldn't have thought any more about this than most women do." She insists that Nature cannot be made the excuse for "ruining the life of a good girl." When she finally confronts him with the question "Do you think it wasn't wrong?" he refuses to answer directly. When he threatens to leave she agrees that he should, and the curtain falls.

Critical Overview--*A Man's World* opened 8 February 1910 at the Comedy Theatre (NY), produced by the Shuberts and staged by Crothers. It played 71 performances, having toured extensively before the New York opening (P4.1). It was made into a film by Metro in 1918. From the beginning the play aroused controversy over its bleak presentation of the double standard of sexual morality; while many commentators found it a stimulating and accurate picture, others found it annoying and uncomfortable. In Philadelphia members of the clergy were invited to attend the play's opening night free of charge (R044), and in Detroit the *News-Tribune* offered 18 pairs of free tickets to women readers for the opening night (R034). An article in the *New York City Review* (R043) mentioned the positive reaction of many members of the local clergy, quoting several letters written in response to the play. However one playwright, Augustus Thomas, was so angered by what he considered an unfair picture of men that he wrote his own play, *As a Man Thinks*, which was produced in 1911, as a rebuttal to Crothers.

A Man's World was also revived for a month's production by the Meat & Potatoes Co., New York, in 1985 .

The reviewer for *Everybody's Magazine* (R038) praised the controversial subject of *A Man's World* but criticized its confusion of character and "a certain absence of strength." *Theatre Arts Magazine* (R049) called it wholesome and defended Crothers's demand for a single standard of morality between men and women. Mary Mannering, in the lead role, was singled out for especially strong praise, and for having discarded "mere prettiness" for depth of feeling in her acting. Ada Patterson in *The Theatre Magazine* (I048) quoted Crothers at length on the necessity of the playwright's having the "courage of the unhappy ending" in order to develop relevant social material on the stage. She described Crothers as a realistic dramatist who knows that one or two plays will not change the world, but who nevertheless intends to present the public with serious, thought-provoking *dramas.*

The Nation (R033) and the *New York Times* (R039) both praised the relevance of the moral points made in the play, although the *Times* reviewer concluded that even plays like this would never alter the fact that this really is "a man's world." *The Nation* was particularly impressed by Crothers's courage in presenting this controversial topic so objectively and candidly. The *New York Daily Tribune* (R040) was one of the few entirely negative voices, complaining that the play was obvious and one-sided, that Mannering's acting was unconvincing, and even criticizing the audience for being too easily pleased.

The *Cincinnati Inquirer* (R042) praised the production in that city, finding it entertaining if not entirely convincing, and especially praising Mannering's strong acting. The tone of the review is somewhat condescending, however, claiming that Crothers takes up the age-old problem of relationships between the sexes but oversimplifies the issues and takes entirely too pessimistic a viewpoint. It also suggests that Crothers seems to think that she has had the last word on this subject.

The Philadelphia production, which opened 10 April 1910, elicited thoughtful comment from the *Record* (R044), which praised it as being "in no sense a sermon" yet conveying a moral message which "has pleased ministers in many cities." The *Philadelphia Times* (R041), however, found it "unnatural," stating that a woman is "apt to let her heart rule her head and hand out only forgiveness...instead of the condemnation she herself knows she should give."

The Chicago *Record* (R037), reviewing the production which opened there on 11 May 1910, agreed that the play was weak, finding only "routine phrases of an ancient argument" in a story which was "improbable." Idah McGlone Gibson (R036), however, responding to the Chicago production, called Crothers "perhaps the best woman dramatist we have today." She praised the realism and truthfulness of the play, citing audience comments as proof. One man, she said, whispered to his companion "It's a deucedly uncomfortable play," while a woman behind her commented, "How men will hate this play, and how women will love it."

Attesting to the timeless quality of the questions raised by *A Man's World*, The Meat and Potatoes Co. revived the play in December 1985 at the Alvin Krause Theatre, directed by Neal Weaver. Steven Steinberg began his review in *Stages* (R283) by pointing out that in 1909 the play was a "daring departure"; however in the contemporary world he found "the story of a woman having to work under a man's name" cliched. Steinberg also complained about the play's ethnic stereotypes, but finally called the production "an interesting period piece," mentioning the receptiveness of the audience.

The film version of the play starred Emily Stevens, John Merkyl and Frederick Truesdell. "Baby Ivy Ward," Metro's four-year-old star, played Kiddie, with Lucille Dorrington as his mother. As this cast suggests, the story was changed somewhat from the play; Frank's stay in Paris and her friendship with Alice were developed at length. The film was generally favorably reviewed, winning praise as a satisfying drama and an uplifting and edifying motion picture.

Since Crothers's observations about the double standard seem mild enough to readers of the late twentieth century, it is worth noting the response to Augustus Thomas's *As a Man Thinks*. Heralded by William Winter in the May 1911 *Harper's Weekly* (R050) as "a great play greatly acted," it was pronounced a "permanent addition to the practical resources of the stage." Winter also quoted John Mason, the lead actor, who praised his role because Dr. Seelig (the character he plays) "*makes a point that has never been made before*" (italics in original), the fact that "the whole structure of modern society rests on man's faith in woman's virtue." Winter praises both Mason and his role in the play for the eloquence with which this point is made, "controverting the impulsive assertion of an excited woman, naturally and rightfully resentful of the injustice often shown toward her sex, that *this is a man's world*, and declaring the essential fact that, in our society at any rate, *this is a woman's world*." Winter added his own feelings on this point: "As long as woman is pure and man continues to worship her, society is safe and civilization will continue to advance." He pronounced Thomas's play "true philosophy" in its suggestions about marriage and the relation between the sexes.

The *New York Review* (R032) said Thomas's play made the entire season worthwhile, contributing to the developing native tradition of the American theatre. The play was called "as fine an achievement in playmaking as the

English-speaking theater has recently produced," and the review predicted that Thomas's dramatic output would be among the most significant contributions of the century.

While most reviews were overwhelmingly favorable, one or two critics disagreed. The "Music and Drama" column in *Current Literature* (R031) praised the seriousness of Thomas's effort, but said he failed to "face the truth squarely and bravely," and that the play suffered from the author's conviction that "the function of the playwright is that of the preacher." The critic also "begged to differ" from the New York critics when they placed Thomas in the "front ranks of American playwrights."

Ourselves (1913)

The Characters--FLORENCE, HARRIETTE and MISS CAREW: employees of a New York City reform school for "wayward girls"; BEATRICE BARRINGTON: a wealthy young woman bent on reforming girls who have been less fortunate than she; MOLLY: a "bit of human jetsam," a reform school inmate chosen by Beatrice for her experiment in philanthropy; SADIE, STELLA, LENA, MABEL, ROSIE, KITTY, LEEZA, CLARA, LETTIE and MARY: other inmates of the reform school, each with a pathetic tale of helplessness and victimization; BOB BARRINGTON: Beatrice's brother, who takes advantage of Molly after Beatrice has befriended her; IRENE BARRINGTON: his rather frivolous wife; LEEVER: Molly's underworld lover who deserts her when she needs him; COLLIN FORD: Beatrice's fiance.

Plot Summary--ACT I. The setting is the parlor of a reform school for girls in New York City, a bleak, cheerless place which the girls try to enliven by quarrelling, dancing, joking and discussing their circumstances with as much comedy as they can. Beatrice Barrington listens to their stories, which, taken together, form an eloquent plea for an equal standard of morality between men and women, since all the girls have in one way or another been victimized by their sex. As Molly explains why a girl might stick to a man even when he drives her to the streets and takes her money--because "he's somebody to come home to"--Beatrice decides to put her theories into practice. She will take Molly under her roof for a month, show her a better way of life, and let her choose which path she would like to follow.

ACT II. The Barrington home. Molly is obviously enjoying good treatment and a good life with the Barringtons, as well as the regard of Beatrice and her friends. When her month is up and her former lover, Leever, comes to claim her, she is angered when he refuses to consider leading a straight, respectable life. She refuses to return to him. At this point, however, stranded in a new life whose ways she has not yet mastered, she meets Bob Barrington, Beatrice's brother, a charming but irresponsible young man who takes his marriage vows lightly. She does not know he is married, and he doesn't seem to care, and the two fall passionately in love.

ACT III. In the month between Acts II and III, Molly has become Bob's mistress. The entanglements multiply when it is revealed that Bob's wife, Irene, is pregnant with their first child, an experience which is transforming her from a rather frivolous, idle socialite to a woman of increasing depth and strength. The inevitable confrontation occurs with great dramatic intensity as Molly begins to realize both what she has done and what has been done to her. Bob discards Molly but Irene still rejects him, vowing she will never see him again after his infidelity (but leaving the audience with the impression that she might not live up to her vow). Beatrice is shattered by both Bob's and Molly's betrayal of her trust. Molly, as the curtain descends, weeps hysterically and asks herself why women "stand for" the tragedies men cause for them.

ACT IV. In Bob's studio. The intensity of Act III is maintained here, as the principal characters express themselves on the subject of men and women and their responsibilities to each other. Bob tries rather lamely to argue that a "respectable" man might be able to keep a mistress without damaging his love for his wife, but he fails to convince Irene, who refuses to have anything more to do with him. Molly, who has heard all sides, comes to a new understanding of her situation and her rights. She promises to teach other girls the things she has learned, and the play ends with a sense of her hard-won independence and self-respect.

Critical Overview--_Ourselves_ (originally called _When it Strikes Home_ and renamed before its Broadway opening) opened on 13 November 1913 at the Lyric Theatre (NY), staged by Crothers and J.C. Huffman. It played 29 performances (P5.1).

Critical response was generally positive, finding the play a strong, intelligent, uncompromising statement on a subject generally considered taboo. The acting in the principal roles, especially that of newcomer Grace Elliston as Molly, was praised by all the critics.

The seriousness with which Crothers's message was received is underlined by the fact that the play was produced at the Bedford State Reformatory for Girls, under the sponsorship of Dr. Katherine Davis, a crusader for prison reform, in December 1913. An interview (I053) quotes Crothers as calling this experience the "most impressive" thing she had ever seen, watching "the agony and shame in 360 faces" and realizing that these girls had gone through some of the same experiences she had captured in her play. She was especially moved by "the respect and throbbing interest" of this very special audience.

The _New York Times_ (R055) called _Ourselves_ better than other contemporary plays on similar subjects; although a bit preachy, its message flowed "naturally from the situations," and the play made its complex moral points with force and eloquence. The review did question, however, whether playgoers might be tired of problem plays of this nature.

Theatre Magazine (R054) praised the play for its excellent construction and for its frankness in handling "facts and conditions as they are." The play is not "meant to please, in any sense of idle enjoyment," but for that reason it succeeds in conveying its "feminist" message, the review concluded. The _New York Evening Journal_ (R056) especially commended Crothers on her courage in presenting such a realistic, convincing presentation of a crucial modern issue which more timid people preferred to ignore. The *New York Tribune* (R057) agreed, commenting on the audience, which sat "spellbound" for four long acts, then burst into tumultuous applause when the play was over. Crothers was praised both for the seriousness of her message and for her skill in translating this difficult material into drama.

Young Wisdom (1914)

The Characters--JUDGE HORACE CLAFFENDEN: as his name and title suggest, a somewhat severe, authoritarian man of 50 who hides his love for his family under a dictatorial manner; ALICE: his wife, 43, a pretty, affectionate woman; VICTORIA: their older daughter, 21, a sweet, pretty, poised young woman; GAIL: their younger daughter, 19, impulsive, impetuous and intense; BARRY: their son; CHRISTOPHER BRUCE: attracted to Victoria; a pleasant young man, but, for 27, rather careful and stuffy; PETER VAN HORN: Gail's fiance, also a bit cautious; MAX NORTON: an artist, 30, a tall, independent, outdoorsy, all-American type; JEAN: Max Norton's French manservant.

Plot Summary--ACT I. The scene is the Claffendens' living room, a chaos of gifts, fabric and clutter marking the preparations for Gail's wedding tomorrow. Gail, however, thinks all this materialism and ritual is old-fashioned and barbaric; very much the modern young woman, she is given to making daring statements about trial marriages and other shocking possibilities. She is even a bit dubious about Peter, fearing he's too stuffy and conventional for her. In short, she is a classic example of pre-wedding jitters, and is threatening to call the whole thing off. Her sister Vic, just home from college, assures her she could never be an old-fashioned, "slavish" wife, and insists that Peter is a very nice young man.

After much conversational soul-searching Gail challenges Peter to prove his love, and his modern attitude, by running away with her. They can get married on the road, Peter suggests nervously, but Gail will have none of this--she wants a trial marriage. Peter is shocked but agrees reluctantly. Vic and Christopher become involved in the argument, and, when Christopher challenges what he considers her newfangled nonsense, Vic issues the same challenge Gail did. All four young people sneak out to make their romantic getaway, at least three of them filled with misgivings about the whole idea.

ACT II. Inside Max Norton's country house, later that same night. A commotion outside suggests an auto accident or some such mishap. Gail and Peter, somewhat disheveled, enter and report that their car went into a ditch; they are followed shortly after by Vic and Christopher, who suffered the same fate. Max agrees to put them up for the remainder of the night and offers sandwiches and drinks. When Gail discovers he is an artist she assumes that he is also a free-thinker, but soon realizes this is not the case. They talk animatedly and it becomes evident that they are attracted to each other, although Max is bewildered by Gail's advanced ideas. Max disapproves of Peter, assuming that he is taking advantage of Gail, and snarls "You ought to be shot." A fight ensues, but Peter finally convinces him that the whole idea of running away together came from Gail. This provides an opportunity for a discussion of changing mores, woman's place in the new society and other contemporary issues. There is also much comic confusion about the sleeping arrangements, and it becomes clear that none of these young people is really convinced of the validity of trial marriages, but no one has the courage to admit it. Confusion is rampant as Peter suggests that they should get married after all, Gail indignantly refuses, and Christopher proposes to Vic, who doesn't want to marry either. Max is the only one who is not confused: he demands that Gail either go home or go to the next town to be married. She refuses.

ACT III. At the Claffendens' at 4 o'clock the same morning. The Judge is distraught, accusing his wife of being too soft with the girls and thus causing the present disaster (about which he is only guessing). The young people, accompanied by Max, enter, and the ensuing argument is comic in its exaggerations and confusion. The Judge isn't interested in explanations; he knows only that his daughters have "been out all night with three men." Vic finally confesses that she has had second thoughts about "modern" ideas but Gail too has had a change of mind--she doesn't want to marry Peter at all. Arguments, accusations and explanations abound. When the smoke finally begin to clear Max professes his love for Gail, who seems to return it; Vic, impressed by the suddenness and depth of this emotion, announces to the pleased Christopher that she loves him. The two couples kiss.

In a whirl of activity Gail, who has escaped from the room in which her father had locked her, admits that she loves Max and agrees to marry him; Vic and Christopher decide to do the same thing, and a relieved Peter volunteers to drive them. The comic climax occurs when Mrs. Claffenden, who has hitherto been only a foil for her domineering husband, offers to come along as chaperone. The suggestion is that she might not be in any hurry to return, and the curtain closes on general merriment.

Critical Overview--_Young Wisdom_ opened 5 January 1914 at the Criterion Theatre (NY) to generally favorable reviews, especially for the Taliaferro sisters, who played the lead roles. It played 56 performances and toured extensively (P6.1). In October 1914 the play traveled to London.

Theatre Magazine (R074) called _Young Wisdom_ "one of the most agreeable plays of the season," praising Crothers's "light, refined touch" and her "feminine delicacy." The review especially lauded Crothers for taking a serious idea appropriate to a "problem play" and instead turning it into comedy. The _New York City Press_ (R062) delighted in the hilarious comedy, especially enjoying the "wholesome preachment" included in the fun. The play was called "the greatest joke of the theatrical season," since the lighthearted comedy was so unexpected from Crothers in the light of her recent serious efforts. The _Times_ (R058) praised both the play and the acting of the Taliaferro sisters, mentioning the enthusiasm and enjoyment of the audience. Algernon St. John-Brenon, in the _New York Telegram_ (R069), especially praised the play for lampooning the pomposity of self-proclaimed "experts" in the field of human behavior who in fact know nothing outside of a little textbook learning. He pronounced it a delightful, exhilarating evening of theater.

The *Boston Transcript* (R073) and the *Atlanta Journal* (R078), reviewing the tour, praised the play's delightful, uproarious humor and its clever satire of modern ideas about free love. Both papers mentioned the enthusiastic audiences which greeted the play, and both praised the playwright for supporting solid values rather than sophisticated notions of morality.

The Philadelphia *Public Ledger* (R072) took a more negative view, calling the play a "maladroit...revolt against the restricting and prosaic properties of old-fashioned matrimony" which failed to "advance effective arguments" against what it presents as "obsolete features of holy wedlock." It found the play conventional and its humor obvious.

The Heart of Paddy Whack (1914)

The Characters--DENNIS O'MALLEY: a personable but somewhat impractical Irishman, a lawyer in an Irish village; MONA CAIRN: his young ward, just returned from school; MISS MARGARET FLINN; an unmarried neighbor, secretly in love with Dennis, publicly more or less in charge of running his household since he has no wife; GRANNY and MICHAEL: poor neighbors seeking justice from Dennis; SQUIRE LINNERING: Dennis's wealthy and powerful neighbor; LAWRIE LINNERING: his son, in love with Mona; MR. and MRS. O'DOWD and MR. and MRS. MCGINNIS: Dennis's neighbors, loudly "at law" against one another; BRIDGET O'REILLY: his servant.

Plot Summary--The setting is the cottage (Acts I, III) and garden (Act II) of Dennis O'Malley, in a small town in Ireland in 1830. ACT I: The curtain rises on an empty room. Granny and Michael, her grandson, enter, loudly demanding O'Malley's help in finding a lost cow. They are rushed out by Bridget; she, Margaret and Dennis discuss the imminent arrival of Mona, who is just home from school. Then Mona enters, bubbling happily about "Uncle Dennis," her happiness at being home, her joyful anticipation of redecorating the faded cottage (she thinks she's an heiress but the audience discovers that Dennis has been spending his own rather scanty funds to keep her from realizing that her parents, his great friends, had died penniless.) Margaret clearly disapproves of Mona and Dennis's mutual fondness for each other; she is more than a little jealous, realizing, though they do not, that their feeling is more than just paternal affection and gratitude.

Enter Squire Linnering, asking Dennis about a property controversy with a Widow Duveen; he is a forceful, domineering type and it is clear that right is probably not on his side. His son Lawrie joins them; he is obviously the appropriate love-interest for Mona--tall, good-looking, not especially intelligent but likeable. They flirt a bit, but Mona is unsure of her feelings. When the Linnerings leave the conversation reveals the source of the phrase "Paddy Whack": When Mona was a baby Dennis would playfully lift his finger and threaten to give her a "paddy whack," and the phrase has become part of their lives and their memories.

ACT II: Two months later. Lawrie and Mona have been playing tennis. He is clearly in love with her, she is clearly doubtful about the whole question. When they leave Dennis and Margaret enter, discussing Dennis's real financial problems. He refuses to let Mona know she isn't really an heiress, but Lawrie's courtship complicates the issue because Squire Linnering will certainly want to know Mona's expectations. Various neighbors seek Dennis's legal advice during Act II, making it clear that part of the reason for his poverty is his generous reluctance to charge his clients for his services. Aided by Margaret, Dennis finally begins to realize that his feelings for Mona are more than fatherly; this horrifies him, however, since he's afraid he's too old for her, and thinks she loves Lawrie. He resolves to say nothing and act only in her best interests.

ACT III. After a turmoil of romantic, familial, neighborly and legal entanglements, love finally wins out. Both Dennis and Mona think their beloved loves someone else; both are finally disabused of this notion; both finally realize the other returns their love. Dennis's honor is saved in Squire Linnering's eyes and the legal questions are answered with justice triumphing; even Lawrie, though disappointed in Mona's love, will clearly not mope for long. The curtain falls on an embracing Dennis and Mona and a thoroughly happy ending.

Critical Overview--*The Heart of Paddy Whack* opened at The Grand Opera House (NY) on 23 November 1914. Reviews were generally favorable, especially praising Chauncey Olcott's graceful transition from youthful heroics to more mature roles. It played 25 performances (P7.1). It was revived in March 1934 by the Irish Drama League, in honor of St. Patrick's Day.

The *New York Times* (R061) called the play the best in which Olcott had ever appeared, praising it for featuring the popular actor throughout the entire play. The *New York Telegram* (R065) was less enthusiastic, calling the story "inconsequential" and warning that those who did not "appreciate Mr. Olcott's plays" would dislike this one. The review went on to say, however, that anyone "so calloused" that he did not like the "obviously clean fun" of the play "does not belong to the work-a-day world," but should be "transplanted to the sphere of the philosopher, the sophist and the bonehead."

The *Brooklyn Eagle* (R068) praised Olcott lavishly, emphasizing his popularity which has "shone undiminishingly through all manner of plays, seasons almost without number." The review especially praised Olcott for leaving his "dashing, romantic, heroic" image and having the courage to play a middle-aged man.

Before opening in New York the play was seen in Baltimore, a production which the *Washington Evening Star* (R059) called it delightful, praising both Crothers and Olcott for letting the star age gracefully and successfully. *Variety* (R067) especially praised the acting, not only of Olcott but also of Edith Luckett as Mona. The *Rochester* (New York) *Post Express* (R060) praised the performance at the Lyceum Theatre lavishly: "It would be difficult to say when Mr. Chauncey Olcott has had so pretty a play [or a role] in which he has appeared to better advantage." The *Hartford* (Conn.) *Courant* (R066) called the play bright and clever, with "quaint turns of fanciful speech and a story that is clean," but found it too long and too predictable. Virtually all the reviews commended Crothers on providing such a successful, delightful vehicle for a popular star.

"Old Lady 31" (1916)

The Characters--ANGIE and ABE: an elderly couple, still very much in love but fallen on hard times; they are forced to separate, she to go to a home for old women, he to the poor-farm; ABIGAIL: the matron of the Home; MRS. HOMANS: a rather pompous resident of the Home, refusing to admit she is no longer a prosperous matron; SARAH JANE: the hard-working, plain-spoken maid; BLOSSY: a faded but still coquettish and giddy resident of the Home, courted by SAMUEL DARBY but reluctant to consent to marry him; MARY: a young woman of a good family who is a volunteer worker at the Home; JOHN: an honest and hard-working young man whose courtship of Mary is discouraged by Mary's father because John is poor; MIKE: a "woman-hating gardener" at the Home; NANCY, ELIZABETH, MINERVA and GRANNY: other residents at the Home.

Plot Summary--PROLOGUE. The time is 1860, the place the charming, well-tended, garden of Abe and Angie's home. The old couple are saying a sad farewell to their home and each other; Abe (once a "fine figure of a sea-captain" but now old and bent) has invested unwisely and he is leaving for the poor-farm. Their last $100 went to buy Angie's way into the Old Ladies Home. Angie is weeping quietly as the curtain falls.

ACT I. The veranda of "The Home." Nancy, Mrs. Homans, Sarah Jane, Abigail and Blossy discuss Angie's imminent arrival. They feel sorry for Angie, who must be separated from her beloved Abe (the rest are spinsters or widows); someone proposes bending the rules and letting him stay. Blossy volunteers to sacrifice her big room for the two of them, and they decide to call him "Old Lady 31," since there are already 30 old ladies in the Home and no men are allowed.

John and Mary enter. They are in love, but since he's a poor, aspiring architect her parents disapprove.

ACT II. All the old ladies are in a flutter over Abe, flattering him, giving him little tidbits, asking his advice. Blossy consults with him about her suitor, Samuel; Abe suggests that, if she doesn't marry him pretty soon (after 20 years' courtship) somebody else will. All blushes, Blossy agrees; not, however, before making the other ladies, who have seen part of this conversation, suspicious of Blossy and Abe. The ladies gossip, beginning to turn against Abe; Angie, who warned him about being everyone's favorite, fears (rightly) that they'll turn him out of the Home. She comes up with a pretty little scheme; she pretends that she had been jealous, but that, when Blossy's engagement was revealed, she felt relieved. Everybody agrees that it would be silly to distrust Abe, and the act ends happily.

ACT III, Scene I. Abe is ailing; Samuel Darby suggests there are too many women nattering over him, and carries him off for some male companionship. When Mary finds Abe's note she weeps, confessing to Mary that he "ain't coming back."

ACT III, Scene 2. A storm rages outside; it is 5 a.m. Angie, a "little huddled miserable figure," stares out the window as Darby comes in, all bedraggled; he doesn't know where Abe is, nor does John. (A subplot is also developing here. Mary has been forbidden to go to the Home, because she'd been meeting John there; John has announced he's going to Boston to make his fortune.)

Suddenly a huddled figure is discovered under a blanket on a couch; it's Abe. Not only is he back, humbly grateful for a good home again, but a letter has been remembered (it came while he was gone). Apparently his investments weren't so bad after all; he is informed that his "Tenafly gold stock" is worth $10.00 a share, and he has eight hundred shares. With these riches they will buy their old house back, help John and Mary get started, and in general live happily ever after.

Critical Overview--The play opened 30 October 1916 at the 39th Street Theatre (NY), produced by Lee Kugel. It played 160 performances, and was received with overwhelming approval by nearly all the critics (P8.1).

Theatre Magazine (R088) praised the play extravagantly, calling it "real, human and charming," mingling "humor and pathos with never a false note." The review praised "the most amazing and amusing aggregation of character types imaginable," but found the juvenile leads, both as written and played, "a jarring note." The reviewer was ecstatic about the star, Emma Dunn, however: "And Emma Dunn--the star--as Angie! Melting voice, winsome personality, splendid art--if there's anybody on the stage lovelier than Emma Dunn, I want to see her."

Heywood Broun in the *New York Tribune* (R081 and R082) and Charles Darnton in the *Evening World* (R083) were also delighted by the play, especially relishing its well-controlled sentiment. A lengthy interview in the *New York Times Magazine* (I085) praised Crothers's direction of *"Old Lady 31"* and quoted her extensively on the future of American theater. Another substantial illustrated article, this one in the Sunday *Herald* (R086), was lavish in its praise of the play's moral values and sentimental enjoyment. The *Times* (R089) also praised Crothers's control of emotional material, while Louis DeFoe in the *World* (R084) praised her skill in both casting and directing, calling this one of the best plays of the season.

Howard Mullin (R087) agreed, warning cynics that they had better be prepared to weep in this delightful, heartwarming play of outstanding moral values. Louis Sherwin, in the *Globe and Commercial Advertiser* (R091), echoed Mullin when he confessed that he had not expected to like any play whose acton "takes place mostly in an Old Ladies Home." He was completely won over, however, by the play's genuine and heartfelt emotion, buoyant humor and skillful dialogue. Like most other reviewers, Sherwin pronounced *"Old Lady 31"* one of the season's major hits.

Mother Carey's Chickens (1917)

The Characters--MOTHER CAREY: the widowed mother of four children, the "chickens" of the title; a wise, loving, consummately maternal woman; NANCY CAREY: the oldest daughter, a lovely, mature young woman who is very close to her mother and who strives to live up to her high standards; GILBERT CAREY: a boy of 16 who is trying hard to take his father's place as "man of the house"; KATHLEEN: the younger sister, a good sport about hand-me-down clothes and tight budgets; PETER: an adorable 5-year-old; COUSIN ANN CHADWICK: a crusty but soft-hearted woman who loves the Careys but disapproves of their impracticality; JULIA CAREY: a young cousin, a spoiled and snobbish girl who is entirely unlike her loving, happy-go-lucky relatives; TOM HAMILTON: the young man whose inheritance threatens to evict the Careys from their new home; OSSIAN POPHAM: a tart-tongued neighbor; MRS. OSSIAN POPHAM: his wife, and equally a New England "character"; LALLIE JOY POPHAM: their daughter; RALPH THURSTON: a helpful neighbor who falls in love with the whole family, but especially Nancy; CYRIL LORD: an unhappy neighbor boy whose artistic ambitions are frustrated by his father's insistence that he be a scholar; HENRY LORD, PH.D.: Cyril's father, a rather aloof man whose chilly relationship with his son is worsened by the fact that his wife is dead.

Plot Summary--ACT I: The setting is The Yellow House in Beulah, New Hampshire, on "an April afternoon in the present." Ossian Popham is helping the Careys move in to the rambling old house they have just bought. Having purchased the house they have no money left, but are brave, optimistic and strongly attached to each other. All the children are determined to succeed in their new home, which their father had chosen for them before he died. They are joined by Cousin Ann, who is more concerned about financial reality than Mother Carey and the children; also by Cousin Julia, who does not know that her father's improvidence caused the Careys' father to lose his money, and thus the family's present plight.

Mrs. Popham and her daughter, Lallie Joy, who is "slow" but charming and droll, provide local color and comic business. Ralph, a local school teacher, is instantly smitten with the entire family, especially Nancy.

As Cyril and Nancy investigate the new home they discover a mural underneath all the old wallpaper. They vow to save it, and Cyril reveals that he wants to be an artist like his dead mother, although his father wants him to be a scholar.

Later Gilbert and Nancy discover, in an old stove, a note to Tom Hamilton from his now-dead grandmother, leaving him the Yellow House as a 25th birthday present. Nancy knows only that Tom is a member of the family from whom they bought the house, obviously knowing nothing of the will. They decide to keep it a secret for the time being.

ACT II, Scene 1. The same house, a month later. Everyone is involved in putting the finishing touches on a room which is still shabby but now warm and lovely, featuring the mural that Cyril has beautifully retouched. They're trimming the room for a party for the neighbors. Ralph is still smitten with Nancy, who seems to return his affection; Julia, as well as being bored, seems jealous. Annoyed by her carping and condescension, Nancy finally snaps that her father made their father lose his money. Julia is appalled.

Enter Tom Hamilton, a very pleasant young man about 25 years old, who is instantly taken by Nancy. Tom, who has no idea that he really owns the house, is enchanted with what the Careys have done to it.

ACT II, Scene 2. The same room, a few hours later. A neighborhood party is in full swing, with everyone contributing something. In the midst of the festivities, however, Julia discovers the hidden will; spitefully, she tells Tom, also hinting that Ralph and Nancy are in love. Because she makes it seem that Nancy was hiding the inheritance from Tom, he is understandably chilly, and the act ends with his brusque departure.

ACT III. In the barn of the Yellow House. As she responds to her new neighbors, Mother Carey's love transforms Lallie Joy and makes Dr. Lord see that Cyril must be allowed to develop his talent. Under her influence, Julia is beginning to feel guilty; she confesses to Nancy that she meant to make her look bad in front of Tom. She clarifies the situation to Tom, and all is forgiven. When no one can find the will Tom finally realizes that he himself had thrown it into the fireplace earlier, without knowing what it was. The problem of the house is now solved, since Tom and Nancy are going to marry.

The music begins; there is a square dance; and the curtain falls on the happy scene.

Critical Overview--*Mother Carey's Chickens* opened to generally favorable reviews on 25 September 1917 at the Cort Theatre (NY). John Golden was the producer and Ralph F. Cummings did the staging (P9.1). Many critics mentioned the refreshing nature of the material, coming as it did in a time of so much gloom, and most commented on the extent of audience enjoyment. The play ran for 39 performances.

The *New York Herald* (R094) praised it highly, comparing it to the dramatized version of *Little Women*: "Judging by the sympathy and the interest at the opening performance the chickens will roost at the Cort for a long time."

The *New York Evening Journal* (R095) also mentioned the gratified audience, comparing the play to both *Little Women* and *Pollyanna*. This review especially praised the "everyday folk [and] natural, homey surroundings." The *Journal* did mention the slightness of the plot, but found that only a minor defect in a play which was so full of delightful, wholesome entertainment.

The *New York Evening Telegram* (R096) mentioned its "delightful idyllic qualities, offering a welcome change from lurid melodrama and libidinous musical comedy. To be sure, it is saccharine at times." The *Telegram* concluded that "The skillful hand of Rachel Crothers, one of the foremost American dramatists, is shown in this expert dramatization."

The *Brooklyn Eagle* (R098) echoed this sentiment: "The world is just gray and drab enough to welcome a a bit of light and idealism...that is why a large audience evidently enjoyed" the play. This review also compared it to *Little Women*.

The *Hartford* (Conn.) *Post (R100)* was less ecstatic, finding in the play "only a series of pretty scenes, brilliant lines and happy and cheerful sentiment." The entertainment value of the play was praised, but it was found to be too loosely structured and ultimately unsatisfying. Like nearly everyone else, however, this review praised the acting, especially that of Edith Taliaferro. The *New York Times* (R093) was also somewhat reserved inits praise, finding the play sweetly entertaining, but remaining unconvinced about the insistence that all virtue resides in rustic life.

It toured to the Providence (R.I.) Opera House, opening on 18 September 1917. The *Providence Journal* (R097) praised Crothers's ability to transfer the novel to the stage. Despite its "slender plot and simple narrative...the atmosphere fairly drips. It is redolent of New Hampshire, with its yellow houses, picture-painted walls," and other regional details.

In 1938 "Mother Carey's Chickens" was made into a film, directed by Rowland Lee. Although neither Kate Douglas Wiggin nor Crothers was involved in writing the screenplay, the film was based on the novel and the play and remained faithful to the original sources. Critics generally praised the movie for its pleasant, old-fashioned sentiment and for avoiding Hollywood tricks, but found the overall effect a bit sweet and not entirely convincing.

Once Upon a Time (1918)

The Characters--TERRY: a charming, talented but somewhat impetuous young Irishman; PATSY: his orphaned niece, now his ward; JOHN: his generous and ambitious friend; LIZZIE and THE BOY: Terry's servant, and a neighbor; MARY: a young woman with a secret; LENOX: Terry's friend; JACK: his rival; ANNIE: Terry's girl friend.

Plot Summary--ACT I: The scene is a run-down apartment building somewhere in the West. Terry and John are discussing Terry's imminent departure for New York, where he means to develop investments in a valuable machine of his invention--Terry is an inventor who has squandered past chances, but this time he means to succeed. John, who is not wealthy himself, has loaned him $1,000, his last cent, for the venture. Half an hour before the train leaves, Lizzie enters with a new complication: Terry's niece, Patsy, who is already fatherless, has recently been left motherless and has no one to care for her. Somewhat reluctantly, but unable to resist the child's love, Terry volunteers for the job--somehow he will conquer New York and care for Patsy at the same time.

ACT II: A comfortable hotel room in New York. Patsy and Lizzie discuss Terry, who is out; they speak admiringly of his intelligence, his capability and his generosity. They also reveal, however, that the investor whom he seeks is not going to be easy to convince, and they are worried about Terry's chance for success. Mary, a lovely young woman who seeks a job as Patsy's governess, enters; as she talks to Lizzie and Patsy it becomes clear that she is, in some unacknowledged way, a part of Terry's past. When Terry enters, laden with extravagant gifts for Patsy, the sense of a previous bond is intensified but the secret is not revealed. Mary is, however, given the position of governess.

ACT III: A week later, still in the New York apartment. As Mary tells Patsy how important truth, fidelity, kindness and generosity are the audience begins to understand her position; an argument with Jack McMasters, who accuses her of seeking Terry out only because he now stands to make a fortune, confirms our suspicions. Mary and Terry were in love several years ago, but she broke their engagement to marry a man with better prospects; he failed, however, and left her not only impoverished and widowed, but also disillusioned and suspicious. She defends herself against Jack's charges, saying that Terry has no idea of her past or the fact that she is a widow. Mary begins to worry when she discovers that Terry has promised Jack a half-interest in his invention in return for his efforts in promoting it; she mistrusts Jack, and probably for good reason.

As Jack and Terry prepare to meet Stevenson, the investor, Patsy is brought in unconscious; she has been struck down in a traffic accident. Terry refuses to leave her, even though he knows he is sacrificing his chance for success with his invention if he fails to meet with Stevenson.

ACT IV: It is five days later; Patsy is recovering but there is no word from Stevenson. Convinced that his hopes are doomed Terry sells his interest in the invention to Jack for $10,000 before Mary can convince him that Jack is not dealing honestly. Terry soon discovers that he has in fact been cheated, but he also discovers that it no longer matters. When he confesses that he still loves Mary she tells him of her own bitter lessons and of her enduring love for him. While they are not rich they have $10,000, they have a recovering Patsy, and they have each other. Given the play's title, it is not too fanciful to say that they will live happily ever after.

Critical Overview--_Once Upon a Time_ opened at the Fulton Theatre (NY) on 15 April 1918 and played 24 performances (P10.1), having already played with some success at the National Theatre in Washington D.C., where it opened 3 December 1917.

The reviewer for _Theatre Magazine_ (R110) called the play a "sweet comedy full of pathos and sentiment." He saw it primarily as a star vehicle for Chauncey Olcott, giving him an "opportunity to sing some of the Irish ditties that he does so well." The review added that Bonnie Marie, a "marvel of a child," was the real "hit of the evening."

Charles Darnton in the _Evening World_ (R105), like many other critics, praised Olcott for leaving the safe roles that his audience expected of him in order to challenge his abilities, and for succeeding in meeting that challenge.

A Little Journey (1918)

The Characters--JULIE RUTHERFORD: a spoiled young socialite suddenly short of money who is reluctantly taking the train West to live with her brother; JIM WEST: a rugged straight-shooter who runs a camp for recovering alcoholics in Montana; MRS. WELCH: a large, domineering, mature woman much given to ordering others about; LILY: an unsophisticated 18-year-old travelling for the first time; MRS. BAY: her sweet, scatterbrained, slightly deaf grandmother; LEO STERN: a fast-talking salesman; FRANK and CHARLES: college boys; ALFRED BEMIS: Julie's beau, who might have solved her financial problems by proposing, but did not; MR. SMITH: an overbearing, pompous man, the male counterpart of Mrs. Welch; ANNIE: a fragile, overburdened young mother; ETHEL and KITTIE: Julie's catty, snobbish friends who are seeing her off on the train; THE PORTER, FIRST and SECOND CONDUCTOR: train employees.

Plot Summary--ACT I: The setting is in Grand Central Station, inside a sleeping car bound for California. The varied character types establish themselves as the play begins: Mrs. Welch and Mr. Smith squabble over the most desirable space, Lily makes it clear that she is an inexperienced traveler who is embarrassed by her outspoken grandmother, the college boys flirt with her, Leo Stern remains the unflappable New Yorker. Julie's friends reveal that she has been living with her aunt, but has had a falling out with her and is now on her own, going to live with her brother in Montana. Alfred, who might have rescued her by proposing marriage, shows no such inclination, and Kittie and Ethel make appropriately catty remarks behind his back.

When they pull out of the station Julie can't find her ticket. The conductor says she'll have to get off at the first stop; gallant Jim West offers to loan her the $92.50. She is at first horrified, but finally swallows her pride and accepts the loan. As they converse Jim reveals that he's a recovering alcoholic who has gone to Montana where he runs a camp for other alcoholics. Julie is reluctantly persuaded to watch Annie's baby while Annie goes to lunch; clearly, Jim is interested in her.

ACT II: Three days later everyone on the train is now gossiping happily. Annie reveals that she's going to join her baby's father, who may or may not be pleased to see her. She is also obviously in ill health, and asks Julie if she knows someone who could keep the baby. Julie's taken aback; she couldn't possibly, since she'll only have about ten dollars left when she gets to Montana. Julie, too, has her problems, since she has no way to earn a living and isn't sure her brother and his family will welcome her; she needs something to believe in, something to do. These serious notes are contrasted to the continued comic byplay of the other characters when suddenly everything is interrupted by noises, shrieks, turmoil: there has been a train crash.

ACT III. The next day, 5 a.m. on a bleak hillside; Leo, Mrs. Welch and several other passengers, much bedraggled, are hauling themselves to the top of the hill, where they rest. Rescue operations are in process. Lily's leg is injured, several passengers are said to have died; Jim West is described as working harder than anyone else despite a broken arm and shoulder. There is an effective blend of pathos and comedy, especially between Lily, Grandma Bay and Mr. Smith.

Suddenly real tragedy is revealed; Annie is dead and Julie, much against her will, has taken charge of the baby. There is a good deal of comic byplay as Julie tries to convince the other passengers to take the baby, and each gives a convincing reason for refusal, from Smith's horrified gasp of "I'm an unmarried man, Miss," to Mrs. Welch's wondering who would want to adopt an illegitimate child "with all its mother's bad traits." Finally kindness prevails, however. Mrs. Welch suddenly offers to contribute $500 a year toward the baby's upkeep and challenges the others to match it. Jim declares his love and offers to help Julie who, after initially insisting on her independence, gratefully accepts both his help and his love. As the play ends the three are presumably on their way to Jim's Montana home.

   Critical Overview--Produced by the Shuberts, *A Little Journey* opened at The Little Theatre (NY) on 26 December 1918. It moved to the Vanderbilt Theatre on 27 January 1919, where it enjoyed a successful run (P11.1). On 4 February 1919 several New York papers carried ads in which former President William H. Taft is quoted as saying he enjoyed the play immensely, laughing till he cried. It played 252 performances.

   Critical response was generally favorable, although several mentioned that it was not an especially original idea, and several thought it a bit slight.

   In the *New York Tribune* (R101), Heywood Broun wrote "There have been a number of plays this season dealing with the manner in which persons have been made over by the war, but 'A Little Journey' adds another factor...It tells of regeneration by railroad wreck." Calling it a "curious but middling good entertainment" with "much excellent observation of life," Broun ultimately judged it "not altogether satisfying or convincing." "The play is thin, but generally agreeable until it begins to preach."

   In the *New York Daily Mail* (R109), Burns Mantle called it "a homely and human and optimistic study in character...wisely cast and skillfully staged." He praised Crothers as "an author of taste and feeling, a playwright with a purpose...and an admirable technician." He also singled out Estelle Winwood for special praise.

   Theatre Magazine (R119) called the play "a little tenuous for a full evening's entertainment" but praised its "freshness of observation, clean-cut character drawing and dialogue," finding it "snappy, witty and true to life....an entertainment safely to be commended."

   The critic for the *New York Evening World* (R106) called it "by far the finest play Miss Crothers has written since 'The Three of Us,'" praising its humor and "simple human feeling." The *New York Herald* (R107) also commended its emotional dimension, calling it "a big adventure of the soul, all the bigger because of its spiritual simplicity." This critic ended rather fulsomely: "The fortunate spectators didn't want to leave their seats when the performance was over. Instead of the usual hurry to get out and away there was an unusual but natural inclination to linger and applaud gently."

   The *New York Times* (R104) praised the well-realized types and the humor but thought the plot a bit thin. The *Evening Sun* (R111) thought it slight but fun, one of "a stream of plays dealing with regeneration."

   A more negative view was expressed by the *New York Evening Post* (R108), which praised the "clever characterization" but found it "more than a little hackneyed and trivial." Despite reservations about the wandering plot and improbable situations, however, the review added that the audience had obviously enjoyed itself throughout.

A Little Journey toured, with essentially the New York cast (although Estelle Winwood was replaced by Ethel Dane) to the Broad St. Theatre in Newark, N.J., the Princess Theatre in Chicago, and the Shubert Theatre in Detroit.

The play was made into a film, opening at the Capitol Theatre in New York on 2 January 1927. While reviewers generally enjoyed the comedy, the romance and the wholesome moral, several complained that the story had been changed drastically in the move to film. The *Herald-Tribune* (R196) commented that it was "a waste to buy plays and then throw away everything except for the title." The character of Jim West was changed into two, George Manning, played by William Haines, and Alexander Smith, played by Harry Carey. Julie Rutherford was played by Claire Windsor. While the romance and the story of the rich girl who loses her money was retained, there was no train wreck and the romance was emphasized more than the comedy.

The New York Graphic (R198) praised it highly, calling it "a gem," "entertainment par excellence" and "well worth the trouble."

39 East (1919)

The Characters--MADAME DE MAILLY: the tough but understanding woman who runs the boardinghouse at "39 East"; NAPOLEON GIBBS: energetic young go-getter who falls in love with Penelope; PENELOPE PENN: star-struck young girl trying to establish herself as an actress; COUNT GIONELLI: dignified Italian fallen on hard times but reluctant to admit it; American food and wine, for example, appall him, but he makes the best of things; TIMOTHY O'BRIEN: brash young American much given to teasing the more pompous of his fellow lodgers; also interested in Penelope; DR. HUBBARD: another impecunious boarder trying to maintain his dignity; MRS. SMITH: a fluffy, scatterbrained, rather nosey woman not above reporting on what she considers the questionable behavior of her fellow boarders, but fundamentally good-hearted; MISS MAC MASTERS: a tart-tongued, fiercely independent New England spinster; MISS SADIE CLARENCE and MISS MYRTLE CLARENCE: faded, vague, "artistic" twins who talk, dress and think alike--and together; WASHINGTON, EVALINA and ROSA: servants at 39 East; POLICEMAN: officer of the law encountered by Napoleon and Penelope in Central Park. As these descriptions indicate, the cast is presented as a comic collection of types which would be found in a Manhattan boarding house in the early 20th century.

Plot Summary--ACT I: The time is "a few years ago," on a spring morning. The setting is carefully established as a dignified but faded New York residence which is pretending not to be what it is--a boardinghouse. The first act is mainly comic dialogue meant to establish character. Everyone is interested in Penelope Penn. Mrs. Smith, for example, reports that she has been out till twelve o'clock three nights in a row. Audience interest is carefully built for Penelope's entrance, nearly halfway through the first act. She is a fresh, pretty 20-year old who inspires romantic notions in the young men and jealousy in the women.

From the first Napoleon seems interested in Penelope, who is obviously enamored of him but will neither see him tonight nor tell him why she cannot. She reveals that she has left home because her family is large and her parents poor (she means to put her sisters and brothers through college); she seeks a respectable singing career, but is behind in her rent. She and Napoleon agree to meet that evening in Central Park.

ACT II: Later that day, in Central Park. Penelope and Napoleon picnic on the grass. He questions her tenderly; she confesses that her only job is the distinctly non-respectable one of chorus girl at the Variety theatre. Penelope's naivete, ambition, pride and self-respect are all equally evident as she insists that she means to conquer the city and make an independent living without surrendering her virtue.

Napoleon sympathetically offers her a loan which she refuses, "blazing with anger and wounded pride." Then they are seen by a very suspicious Mrs. Smith. Penelope's amusing naivete is evident when she tells Napoleon that some of the chorus girls seem to be better off financially than others, but have only small roles--she can't imagine how they earn the extra money. Napoleon thinks he knows. He vows to help her whether she wants him to or not, because a good girl is "the most helpless thing on earth." She disappears.

ACT III: Back at the boardinghouse. The Misses Clarence are just finishing their recital and everyone is polite but bored. Mrs. Smith gossips about seeing Napoleon and Penelope in the park, and everyone assumes the worst. Penelope enters and tries to pay her rent to Mrs. De Mailly, who is suspicious and worried, but trying to be helpful. She suggests that Penelope should marry Napoleon because he's crazy about her; Penelope refuses indignantly. Eventually she innocently reveals the source of her newfound money: her stage manager asked her to supper. In response to his questions about her career she had confided in him about her family's problems and her own intentions, not only to help them, but to succeed in the theatre. Clearly, her naivete had dissuaded the stage manager from his original intentions, since he put her in a cab, suggested she didn't really want the supper he had offered, and handed her a week's salary which was only the beginning. Because her act had been a hit that night, she would be able to make it on her own.

Both Napoleon and Mrs. De Mailly are impressed with this story. Mrs. De Mailly offers her a room as long as she needs it, and asks Napoleon, as she leaves the room, "Kind of makes you believe in things again, don't it?" Napoleon explains to the puzzled Penelope that seeing miracles often has that effect on people.

Napoleon proposes; she refuses, asserting her love of independence and her career ambitions. He professes his love; she eludes him but she finally agrees that she loves him too. As the curtain falls it is clear that they love each other, but not clear whether she in fact will surrender her ambitions for herself and her family in order to marry immediately. Penelope is still strong-minded and independent. Love will conquer all, but not necessarily right away.

Critical Overview--*39 East* opened to enthusiastic reviews on 31 March 1919. It was produced by the Shuberts and staged by Crothers at the Broadhurst Theatre (NY). On 14 July 1919 it moved to the Maxine Elliott Theatre. It played 160 performances (P12.1).

Nearly all the critics commented favorably on Crothers's exploitation of the comic potential in the types to be found in a New York boardinghouse. Typical of these is the comment by Burns Mantle in the *New York Evening Mail* (R120): "So long as there are innocents abroad there will be boarding houses, and so long as there are boarding houses there will be comedy dramas, not to mention tragedies. And so long as there are dramas and tragedies to be written out of boarding houses, Rachel Crothers is one of the playwrights we prefer should write them." He praises it as a "simple human affair" that "wears thin at the center...but still holds its fast colors and attractive patterns." Constance Binney, of a New York acting family, received special attention; she "plays the role charmingly," with "youth, beauty [and a] captivating smile."

The critic of the *New York Review* (R112) was also captivated by Binney, who had just begun her acting career. He praised her charm, her allure, her prettiness, and predicted great success for her. He also praised the producers for presenting one of the most delightful experiences of the current season. The critic for the *New York Evening World* (R116) was also enthusiastic about Binney, noting that she belonged to a well-known New York family and praising her talent extravagantly. He commented that the play was probably not especially realistic but was a joyous celebration of young love and the possibilities, rather than the probabilities, of success in a career in New York.

The *New York Evening Telegram* (R121) called it a triumph of genuine suspense, with type characters which are "never merely types," and an "adorable little heroine."

Theatre Magazine (R119) was mostly positive, praising the play's presentation of optimistic youth and unabashed sentiment even if it failed to "measure up to the exacting standards of modern dramaturgy." Like nearly all the other reviews, this one too praised Binney.

Not quite so enthusiastic was John Corbin of the *New York Times* (R113), who said its romance produced "an amiable and optimistic mood," but little else. He too praised Binney, however. The *New York Post* (R118) was also less than enthralled, saying the play was "old in form and in much of its material, but often fresh in ideas and treatment." The *New York Globe and Commercial Advertiser* (R123) called it a "naive combination of dime thriller, fairy tale, a novel by David Graham Phillips or Theodore Dreiser." It was pronounced charming but a little too sweet. Allan Dale, of the *New York American* (R115), also found the play too sentimental, "feeble" and naive, but even he agreed that Binney was very effective in the lead role.

39 East also toured, appearing in the Grand Opera House Co. in Wilkes-Barre, Pa., the Little Theatre of Mobile, the Princess Theatre in Chicago and Ye Wilbur Theatre in Boston.

It was revived in Westchester in January 1921. Chester Morris, a drama columnist for *The Examiner*, appeared as Napoleon Gibbs, and the play was generally praised as a good, wholesome comedy which provided its audience with spontaneous fun.

"39 East" was filmed in 1920 with a screenplay by Julia Crawford Ivers. John S. Iverson directed and Constance Binney starred as Penelope.

He and She (1920)

The Characters--ANN HERFORD: a sculptor, "intensely feminine," strong and vibrant; TOM HERFORD: her husband, also a sculptor, vigorous, confident and successful; DAISY: Tom's sister, an unmarried woman whose acceptance of her lot is only a pose; RUTH CREEL: Ann's friend, an unmarried novelist; DR. REMINGTON: Ann's father; KEITH McKENZIE: Tom's assistant, 35, in love with Ruth; MILLICENT: the Herfords' daughter, 16; ELLEN: the Herfords' maid.

Plot Summary--ACT I. The Herfords' studio. Keith and Tom are discussing the problems of two-career marriages. Keith, who clearly wants a traditionally domestic wife, complains that Ruth will marry him only if he lets her continue working; Tom contends that Ann's career presents no problem. When Ann enters she looks at Tom's work, to be submitted in a major competition, and wonders if it isn't a bit conventional, then quickly changes that to the kinder "orthodox." Alone with Ruth she confides that she has a wonderful idea, but doesn't dare suggest it to Tom.

Further conversation reveals that Daisy, who pretends to love her independence, is really embittered because she was too plain to attract a man and she has "settled" for spinsterhood, not chosen it. Ruth also reveals that, despite her love for Keith, she is practical enough to want financial and creative independence for herself as well as for him. "Why can't we both achieve together?" she asks, but he is clearly dubious about that proposition. Dr. Remington reveals that despite his love for his daughter he is convinced that her first responsibility is to her family, not herself; independent women are destroying the sexual relationship in the modern world, he insists. Prodded by all these pressures, including Tom's condescension to her idea for the competition and Ruth's insistence that it has merit, Ann decides to enter the contest on her own.

ACT II. The Herfords' living room. As Ann nervously awaits the results of the competition, she, Ruth and Daisy discuss the gigantic responsibilities of motherhood. Daisy is shocked to discover that Ruth doesn't want the burden of a family and even more horrified when Ruth jokingly suggests that being a mistress would be ideal, since it leaves room for female independence.

When Keith and Ruth discuss the issue of independence they quarrel, and she angrily ends their engagement. Daisy's response makes it clear that she secretly loves Keith, but has no hope he returns the feeling. Then Daisy announces that Millicent's school has called: Millicent has disappeared. They decide not to tell Ann yet, since the girl is probably coming home.

The mail reveals that Tom has not won the competition; under Ann's encouragement, however, he seems to take the disappointment calmly. Things get more complicated when Ann discovers that she *has* won. Embarrassment ensues as everyone congratulates Tom, assuming that he must be the winner; he accepts the situation gracefully, but is clearly uncomfortable. Dr. Remington is less generous when he discovers what Ann has done; he would prefer that she fail "a thousand times over, for your own good," he proclaims, asking her what she intends to do with Millicent while she's "making this thing." Ann unhappily accuses him of being hard and narrow, but he remains adamant. Tom praises her, saying she won because hers was the best design, then exits; Dr. Remington predicts that he will never recover. Ann insists he's a bigger person than that.

As Tom and Ann talk later, it becomes evident that Tom is perhaps less large-souled than Ann had thought. He refuses to touch any of the money she won, accusing her of rejecting Millicent in her concern with herself. At this point Millicent herself enters, announcing that she has quit school and refusing to go back.

ACT III. One-half hour later. Daisy and Ruth discuss Millicent's rebellion, Daisy blaming Ann and Ruth arguing with her. Dr. Remington, talking to Tom, quotes a popular saying: "A woman, a dog and a walnut tree--the more you beat 'em, the better they be." Tom disagrees, but half-heartedly; he is clearly very unhappy. Millicent, too, thinks it's "perfectly horrid" that her mother has won; her father should have it since he's the man, she confides, asking her mother if Tom is hurt by the incident.

Finally Millicent blurts out that she has become engaged. Ann, understandably horrified, asks Millicent to go away with her on vacation; Millicent reluctantly agrees. Ann tells Tom privately that she means to win their daughter away from the boy, asking Tom to take over her sculpture; he refuses. Ann is adamant, however; her daughter needs her, and that's more important than artistic success. Tom warns her that she will hate herself some day; Ann knows that, and suspects that she might also resent Millicent eventually, but she is trapped: if the choice is between her daughter and artistic success, she must give up success. Tom agrees, impressed with her spirit of self-sacrifice; he vows to make it as easy for her as he can, insisting that he understands her suffering. "My God, it's hard!" he exclaims, and they leave together as the play ends.

Critical Overview--*He and She* opened 12 February 1920 at the Little Theatre (NY) and played 28 performances (P13.1). From beginning (written in 1911 and produced in Albany, produced in Boston as *The Herfords* in 1912, then renamed *He and She* and performed on tour in 1917 and 1919 before opening on Broadway in 1920) to end (a revival by the American Theatre Company in March 1971 and another at the Brooklyn Academy of Music (P13.2) in June 1980), however, the play received attention and incited controversy quite out of proportion to the brevity of its run.

Crothers's perseverance in getting it produced at all was a much-told show business story. She had tried numerous producers over a period of ten years before finally succeeding in bringing it to Broadway. Then, when lead actress Viola Allen left the play in its Boston tryout because she found Ann Herford's role too unsympathetic, Crothers herself took the part for the Broadway run. The play's presentation of the problems of career, creativity and motherhood clearly fascinated the critics, yet nearly all of them found Crothers's picture too bleak, her treatment of men too negative.

The reviewer in *The Call* (R129), for example, praised the play's "comedy" but found it unkind to men, "rubbing into the male hide the fact that he is a petty little grub." Both the negative sentiment and the jocular tone were echoed by Alan Dale in the *New York American* (R125). Dale condescendingly wondered why "men--the lazy things," don't bear children, implying that Crothers thinks they should. "Personally, I love these discussions of the he and she problem," Dale concluded. "They are so arch; they are so naive; they are so ingenuous. The emancipation of the lady has set in, and now she's starting to get funny."

Other reviews took *He and She* more seriously but still disliked its message. J. Ranken Towne in the *New York Evening Post* (R136), for example, criticized the play for presenting a too-complicated, insoluble problem, but conceded that the issue was important in the contemporary world. He praised "the genial old doctor, Ann's father," for advising her to sacrifice career to family. Towne also liked the characterization of Daisy, "who has no illusions on the subject of unrestrained feminine liberty, and holds that life has no joys comparable to those of an active, contented housewife and busy, affectionate mother." He found Daisy's "old-fashioned heartiness and simplicity" an "agreeable relief to the sophistical and artificial atmosphere" created by Ann and Ruth and their creative ambitions. The critic for the *Evening Telegram* (R137) agreed, praising the characterization of the "shrewd, kindly old physician" who has his daughter's best interests at heart.

Other critics found the play's resolution too negative and unfair to women. Heywood Broun, for example, was so intrigued by *He and She* that he discussed it at length in his column in the *New York Tribune* (R124). He treated Crothers's ideas seriously, but declared himself "in complete disagreement" with them, protesting an "anti-feminist" tone on the contemporary stage in general. He defended the idea that a woman could combine career and motherhood, arguing that soup "tastes just as good whether it is opened with loving care or by the hired help," and suggesting that "young daughters who become entangled in inappropriate love affairs" are not necessarily saved by mothers who give up everything for them. He praised Crothers's development of her ideas, however, and found her acting, while "sometimes understandably nervous," generally excellent.

Weed Dickenson, in the *New York Morning Telegraph* (R127), also rejected the bleakness of Crothers's picture and made fun of the critics who accepted it. "One can almost hear the gentle sound of soapy dishes sliding down the draining board," he said of the ending, suggesting that a couple as intelligent as Tom and Ann should have been able to find a more balanced solution. He praised the play's structure and dialogue, however, and found the acting absorbing.

The *New York Herald* (R128) also found Crothers unfair to feminism in *He and She*, making her point only by exaggerating her characters. In demanding

SUMMARIES AND OVERVIEWS 45

that a creative mind starve itself to death, Crothers recommends disastrous remedies for a problem which should be solved in other ways, the review concluded. Kenneth MacGowan, in two articles for the *Globe and Commercial Advertiser* (R130 and R131), also expressed a negative view, conceding the significance of the play's "polemic value" but finding thesis plays generally unrewarding both to the audience and to the critics forced to write about them.

Charles Darnton in the *New York Evening World* (R126) made just the opposite point, praising the fairness and restraint with which Crothers presented her arguments. Burns Mantle, in the *New York Evening Mail (R132)*, agreed, praising the realization of her ideas. The unsolved problem is realistic, Mantle contended, since society itself had thus far failed to find a way for women to combine careers with motherhood. Alexander Woollcott, writing in the *New York Times* (R138), was impressed by the "valiant undertaking" represented by *He and She,* praising Crothers for taking the role of Ann and emphasizing the enthusiasm with which the audience responded both to her and to the "intensely provocative" play. Like Mantle, Woollcott praised Crothers's somber conclusion, pointing out that society as it is presently structured leaves little room for women who want to excel in both careers and motherhood.

The review in *Theatre Magazine* (R134) tried to embrace both sides of the argument, insisting that women "can lead public lives" but concluding that "Nobody has ever doubted the right of a woman of genius to follow that genius; but it is the common belief, overwhelmingly justified, that the genius of most women lies at home."

Sixty and 70 years later the questions still had not been answered. Bonnie Moranca, in *Show Business* (R276), reviewed the 1971 revival favorably, finding the play amusing and timely even though its attitudes and devices were dated. Moranca found the play's exploration of a woman's right to work, balanced against her family's right to her love and attention, as absorbing in 1971 as it had been in 1910. "Things haven't changed much these past 60 years," she concluded.

The 1980 revival at the Brooklyn Academy of Music received a good deal of attention despite mixed reviews. In the *Daily News* (R286) Douglas Watt praised the play's candid approach to feminism and its consistency of argument, but found it far too didactic. Crothers was no Ibsen, Watt concluded. Mel Gussow in the *New York Times* (R270) agreed, stating that the once-daring Crothers seemed conventional and repetitious 60 years later. Steve Lawson in the *Soho Weekly News* (R274) also found the content dated, but praised the attempt as a presentation of "period Americana."

Erika Munk of the *Village Voice* (R277) was less kind, calling Crothers a "middle-class snob" and charging that the play "trivializes the real difficulties and torn allegiances" of an attempt to combine motherhood and a career. John Simon (R281) agreed with this indictment, calling the play conventional and manipulative, illustrating a "basic incomprehension of what a true artist...is all about--not surprising coming from a successful boulevard playwright."

More positive reviews appeared in *Variety* (R271), which found parts of *He and She* "as strong as almost anything in Ibsen," and the *Christian Science Monitor* (R284), which praised the BAM Theater Company for their "ongoing search for good but 'forgotten' plays," and found *He and She* surprisingly contemporary, comparing it to the recent film "Kramer vs Kramer." Edith Oliver of *The New Yorker* (R278) agreed, finding it "sound and funny and not a bit dated."

In the *New York Post*(R282) Marilyn Stasio praised the production at length, emphasizing its contemporary relevance. Calling it a "brand-new feminist play that happens to be 70 years old," Stasio found its freshness startling. "Entire lines from this play are probably being spoken at this very moment," she contended, "at Weight Watchers meetings, in the dressing rooms in Bloomie's, in the checkout lines at Zabar's and in beds throughout America." Stasio was especially interested in Crothers's posing the question of how much success a woman was permitted before her loved ones, her community and even her own guilt destroyed her, concluding that the question Crothers raised 70 years ago is still unanswered by the women's movement.

Women's Wear Daily (R272) also took the play seriously, calling it a thought-provoking reminder that feminists 70 years ago were asking exactly the same questions they are today. Zoe Kaplan in *Other Stages* (R273) praised the play's timeliness and hard-mindedness in ending with a choice that made critics and audiences as uncomfortable in 1910 and 1920 as it does in 1980, pointing as it did to "the flaw in society which necessitated such choice."

Nice People (1921)

The Characters--THEODORA "TEDDY" GLOUCESTER: A wealthy, motherless young woman, very modern and rebellious, trying to find herself in Post-World War I America; HUBERT GLOUCESTER: her father, well-intentioned and loving but clearly unable to control her; MARGARET RAINSFORD: her aunt, a distinguished, rather weary woman who is appalled by the younger generation and convinced that her son, who was killed in France, gave his life for something better than this; SCOTTY WILBUR: a young socialite in love with Teddy but at least as much in love with her money; TREVOR LEEDS and OLIVER COMSTOCK: young men-about-town; HALLIE LIVINGSTON and EILEEN BAXTER-JONES: Teddy's friends, the picture of flaming youth, clever, catty and rich; BILLY WADE: a young man from the West who is entirely unimpressed by metropolitan decadence; MR. HEYFER: a handyman at Teddy's country place in Westchester.

Plot Summary--ACT I: The setting establishes a mood of New York City luxury--grand piano, fireplace, privileged, well-dressed people. The young people are the picture of decadence and flaming youth; they smoke, drink, sneer at Prohibition and make fun of conventional values. The girls are dressed daringly in the newest fashions, startling in their "delicate nakedness and sensuous charm." (In terms of tone it is worth noting that Hallie and Eileen were originally played by Tallulah Bankhead and Katharine Cornell.) From the first the young people make it clear that they intend to live life in the fast lane. Teddy's Aunt Margaret attacks Hubert, charging that his dead wife Lucille would be horrified to see her daughter "half naked and wearing pearls that no young girl should ever wear." Hubert is convinced that the younger generation is all right, candid and aboveboard; she is appalled by their drinking and smoking, contending that nice young girls are as dependent on cigarettes to calm their nerves as street girls are. Finally her fears convince him and when Teddy returns home from the theatre he forbids her to go out again. She pretends to give in, but the minute his back is turned she escapes with Scotty.

ACT II, Scene 1. 7 p.m. the following evening, at the Gloucester summer cottage in Westchester, a simple old farmhouse room, quaint and chintzy. Scotty and Teddy, who have broken in, are joking about their scandalous behavior. Teddy intends to punish her father, making him wonder what they're up to and where they are. Scotty asks Teddy to marry him, but she is afraid he's after her money, and she is quite possibly right. Scotty falls asleep, to Teddy's displeasure. Suddenly a violent storm breaks out. Billy enters; he too is seeking refuge from the storm. He is a young man from the West, trying to figure out the decadent East. He's fascinated by Teddy but would never take advantage of her. Teddy takes refuge upstairs; Billy and Scotty sleep in the living room.

ACT II, Scene 2: Dawn. Mr. Heyfer, the handyman, is horrified to discover trespassers but Teddy tells him they have a right to be there; then he's even more horrified that these young people have spent the night, and none of them married.

Margaret and Hubert enter, distraught and horrified. Teddy is furious at their suspicions; Hubert insists that she marry Scotty to save her reputation. When she indignantly refuses, insisting she doesn't need saving, he tells her he doesn't want her to come home; she says that's fine with her.

ACT II, Scene 3. The next day. Margaret and Teddy have been roughing it on the farm. Rustic humor is provided by Heyfer, who puts no stock in "autimobiles" and other machines of this "infernal age," but Teddy remains unamused, still fuming about the unfairness of the scandal she knows is breaking. Margaret lovingly cautions Teddy not to play with people's emotions too much. They are interrupted by Hallie, Eileen, Oliver and Scotty with all the fresh scandal about Teddy's shredded reputation; Hallie, particularly, is obviously enjoying this immensely.

Finally Teddy breaks down and agrees to marry Scotty--the scandal is too much for her. She knows he loves her money at least as much as he loves her, but she doesn't care. Teddy remains unsentimental, intending to get a divorce "right off the bat" if they don't get along.

Billy protests her decision, but Teddy is adamant--no one will believe her, and if they told everyone that Billy was there to witness her chaste behavior, they'd be even more scandalized. Teddy is discouraged: her rebellion is a failure. Billy challenges her to become independent, to live on this little farm and get along without her father. She is frightened of failure but resolves to try, with Billy's encouragement.

ACT III: The scene, three months later, is bucolic: Eileen is choosing a golf club, Margaret is sewing, and Teddy, in overalls, is enraptured about a hen with a brood of chicks. Clearly Billy and Teddy are in love. Billy doubts Teddy's ability to sustain all this, fearing that she can't resist her father's wealth, and he won't marry her unless she rejects the money. They argue, with Teddy first rejecting her father and his money because he makes her angry, then Billy because he doesn't believe in her. Finally Teddy chooses Billy, explaining that money without love would be meaningless. There is a feminist twist at the end, however, since Teddy takes the initiative and proposes to him, rather than the other way around.

   Critical Overview--Produced by Sam H. Harris and staged by Crothers, *Nice People* opened to an outpouring of critical and public attention on 2 March 1921 at the Klaw Theatre (NY). It was chosen one of the Best Plays of 1920-21 by Burns Mantle and played 242 performances (P14.1). With a script adapted by Clara Baranger it was made into a successful film in 1922.
   While not strictly speaking a part of the critical response, a story from a New York newspaper of 1921 (R146) sheds light on the strength of the public reaction to the issues discussed by the play. The story states that Rabbi Stephen S. Wise electrified his Carnegie Hall Congregation by preaching to them about "the vices of present-day women," finding his theme in Crothers's play.
   Wise began by stating that he rarely took note of Broadway plays, but was moved to comment on *Nice People* because he found it a "startlingly vivid and powerful human document which epitomizes in dramatic form" the message that countless men and women "within and without the pulpit" were trying to communicate to their contemporaries.
   The story adds that "lip sticks, cigarettes, drink, and harlotry" were all discussed by Wise in his effort to disclose the underlying causes of social problems that, he contended, made "the daughters of 'nice people' conform" in their behavior to "the standards set by women of the streets."
   The story continues with Wise's appeal to contemporary women to maintain high standards "in the face of much that is unclean, vicious and malign about them," adding that the lives of future generations would be improved if all young women of leisure and education remembered "the dignity of their calling and the meaning of their enfranchised womanhood."
   Wise blamed the collapse of moral standards on the Great War, as well as a misunderstanding of the meaning of the women's movement. Freedom is not "illimitable indulgence in smoking and drinking" or rowdy behavior, he said, concluding that, in their understandable revolt against a double standard of morality, women should raise the standards of men's behavior, not lower their own.
   In contrast to Rabbi Wise, Alexander Woollcott in the *New York Times* (R170) was amused at the outcry against the shocking behavior of the youth of the day who "drink and smoke and go out till all hours unchaperoned and disgustingly dressed." He praised Crothers for not wringing her hands with most of her contemporaries, but for instead "writing this pointed and genuinely interesting play." He disliked the ending, with its exaggerated faith in simple country virtues, but praised the acting, especially that of Francine Larrimore as Teddy. He also added "a word of praise for the comely and competent Tallulah Bankhead, who luxuriates in a feline role" (Hallie).
   Louis V. De Foe, in the *New York World* (R144), found it "not altogether a

nice play to watch," but a valuable, thought-provoking presentation of the "reckless spendthrifts and aimless habits and diversions" of the day. Echoing the feelings of Rabbi Wise and others, De Foe concluded that "The sadness of Miss Crothers's play...is that it is true." Like Wise, he blamed the Great War for the creating a world in which the "dissipation of these 'nice' young people" would be appropriate for "red-light melodramas" of an earlier age. De Foe also applauded the presentation of the "unrestrained talk, the dancing, the drinking, the smoking, the heedlessness to every delicate propriety of feminine conduct...[which] are unfortunately too faithful to the life that is being presented and jocularly dismissed."

Unlike Woollcott, De Foe's only complaint about the ending is that it throws away a valuable opportunity to preach. "Theodora should pay the penalty of her own perversity" instead of being rescued by a "conventionally moral young man," De Foe concluded.

The New York Tribune (R160) review suggested that the play should be called "The Wild Young People," the title of a recent Atlantic Monthly symposium on the morality of the times. It praised the play for its "keen insight into Teddy," and, like De Foe, approved of its message, calling it one of the season's most delightful plays.

Theatre Magazine (R159) called it a "strong and interesting" play "weakened only by the too common conventionality of its denouement." Crothers "barely escapes preaching but she also reveals, with startling clearness, things which are of common occurrence, not only...in high society...but among the masses." Describing Teddy as a spoiled young thing who is "going the pace with her young friends, dancing, dining, smoking, drinking and swearing," the review concluded that she "needs a chaperone." The acting of Larrimore and Bankhead is praised, as is the new Klaw Theatre in which the play opened. Burns Mantle in the Mail (R154) called Nice People one of the outstanding hits of the season, while Alan Dale in the New York American (R142) was especially enthusiastic about Larrimore's performance.

Charles Darnton in the Evening World (R143) praised the new Klaw Theatre but found the play too sensational in its presentation of Park Avenue life, though generally entertaiing. Robert Benchly of Life (R140) was also largely unimpressed, remaining unconvinced by Crothers's faith in the virtues of rural existence as opposed to city life. Amy Leslie of the Daily News (R152) made just the opposite point, however, finding Crothers's picture of modern life a "brilliant, stinging commentary." An extensive interview-article in the New York Herald (I153) agreed, quoting Crothers extensively on the subject of the dramatist's duty to make moral points while entertaining the audience.

Everyday (1921)

The Characters--JUDGE NOLAN: the domineering but loving father of Phyllis, the domineering and not especially loving husband of Fannie, and very much a man of power; FANNIE NOLAN: his weak, sickly, lovely but spiritless wife; PHYLLIS NOLAN: their independent young daughter, just returned from an extended European visit; MRS. RAYMOND: a friend of the Nolans who thinks her son would be the perfect match for Phyllis; MAY RAYMOND: a friend of Phyllis, a "flapper" who is bored with smalltown existence; T.D. RAYMOND: a former beau of Phyllis's; JOHN MCFARLAN: war veteran and butcher's son, a poor but hardworking young man who means to repeat the Horatio Alger success story; he falls in love with Phyllis.

Plot Summary-- ACT I: An afternoon in October. Decor is important in the play, which is set in the Nolans' living room, a stiff, pompous and uncomfortable room which is "boastfully" decorated. As the play opens the Nolans instantly reveal themselves as an unhappy couple. She's neurotic, hypochondriacal, utterly dominated by him; he's pushy, overbearing and inconsiderate. Phyllis, who has just returned from Europe, is natural, attractive and vital. She's glad to be home, but dubious about her parents' relationship and her mother's illness. She is appalled by the room, which is obviously her father's pride and joy; she asks her mother if she likes it, and mother responds only that "It was very expensive."

When the Raymonds enter it is clear that they are selfish, superficial people. T.D., whose mother firmly intends him to marry Phyllis, is rather weak and hardly worthy of Phyllis; May is much given to slangy dialogue and interested only in Paris fashions. The focus is on Phyllis's future: will she follow her father's dictates or her own inclinations? Her father has chosen Berry Wyman, a wealthy, up-and-coming young politician, as her husband, but Phyllis intends to make her own decisions. Fanny preaches a traditional role for women: put up with what you're sent and get along as well as you can. Phyllis finds this hateful.

ACT II: Six weeks later. When John and Phyllis meet they are equally charmed with each other. John works for the Judge, and is poor but ambitious; Phyllis also discovers that he has artistic talent which he has been trying to ignore.

In a second plot line it becomes clear that both the Nolans and the Raymonds are heavily involved in Wyman's questionable financial doings, which are now being investigated by a local newspaper. Much is at risk, and the differences between morality and expediency are developed, with expediency winning. Phyllis remains idealistic. When she discovers Wyman is in trouble she is reassured that he is innocent; she decides to marry him because she can help him. John is horrified.

ACT III: Two weeks later. A chilly, nervous vigil as Fanny and Mrs. Raymond await news of Wyman's case, which Nolan is now defending in court. They discuss love, marriage, and their hopes for their children, revealing resignation (Fanny) and cynicism (Mrs. Raymond). Both of them, however, suggest that love doesn't always conquer all, that sometimes a woman's sacrifice of both self and self-respect for marriage is more than the marriage is worth.

Finally the news comes that Nolan has won the case. The Raymonds are ecstatic. Winning is not enough for the idealistic Phyllis, however; she insists on asking if right has been done. When no one can reassure her that it has been, there is an argument. Phyllis refuses to marry Wyman and attacks her father for wanting to give her to a thief; John, who is thoroughly disillusioned with politics and wrongdoing, quits Nolan's employ and declares his love for Phyllis. She reciprocates. Horrified at his daughter's rejection Judge Nolan attacks Fanny, blaming her for instilling "picayune" ideas of morality in Phyllis. Phyllis defends her mother; the Judge continues to bluster until Phyllis, saying he isn't her father but only a man who "happens to be married to my mother," storms out.

Nolan is a broken man, but still doesn't understand that he has created the disaster. When Phyllis re-enters, wanting a reconciliation, he graciously offers one if she will change her mind; she refuses. She leaves, stating firmly that she will make it on her own, without her father's money or influence, and that she intends to marry John McFarlan. As the curtain falls the Judge is still staring "with unbelieving helplessness" at the door through which Phyllis has left.

Critical Overview--Produced by Mary Kirkpatrick, *Everyday* opened on 16 November 1921 at the Bijou Theatre (NY). The play was generally well received, and was chosen by Burns Mantle as one of the Best Plays of 1921. It played 30 performances (P15.1).

Crothers did her own casting, a fact worth mentioning in light of the strong critical praise not only for the acting, but also for the perceptiveness and originality of the casting. In fact she can be given credit for "discovering" Tallulah Bankhead, who had her first starring role in *Everyday*. Bankhead had made her first stage appearance as a bit player and understudy in *39 East*. When Estelle Winwood, the star, left for Hollywood, Bankhead played the role of Penelope Penn for a time. Crothers then requested her for the "feline" role of Hallie in *Nice People*, and again for the lead in *Everyday*.

Alexander Woollcott in the *New York Times* (R169) praised the play as "substantial entertainment," only partially original but with a strong cast and sound production. Woollcott was ambivalent; he praised the genuineness of the social commentary but criticized Crothers for failing to take full advantage of her own material. The acting, however, received unqualified praise, especially "the beauteous Tallulah Bankhead," who "quite justified the choice of her for the central role."

J. Ranken Towne of the *New York Post* (R166) also praised the play's strong acting, singling out Bankhead for her "altogether sincere and sympathetic portrayal," although he commented on a "vocal catch" which at times "marred her diction." While he praised the play for its soundness, its realization of potential and for being "on the whole thoroughly good entertainment," Towne expressed "a shade of disappointment" at what he considered the excessive theatricality, the melodramatic elements which distracted from the play's general excellence.

The *New York Evening Telegram* (R148) praised Crothers for having attempted to present realistic versions of everyday life "long before 'Main Street', 'Miss Lulu Bett' and kindred plays." The review compared the heroine to Nora in *The Doll's House*, though it did find Crothers's characters less strong and convincing than Ibsen's. Again Bankhead was singled out, receiving praise for her characterization which was "an embodiment of the girl of the moment." The *New York Evening Journal* (R151) echoed this judgment, praising the casting and acting especially.

While most of the critics enjoyed the play, some found it trite and superficial. Louis V. De Foe of the *New York World* (R144), for example, found it very ordinary, with "no new truths to reveal," if effectively staged and acted. He compared it to a rhinestone in a setting appropriate to diamonds. The review in *Vogue* magazine (R147) agreed, saying that the play's beginning promised a return to Crothers's older, "uncompromising" vision of contemporary society, but that the situations became "spineless and ill-directed." Earle Dorsey, reviewing the Washington production in the *Washington Herald* (R145), attacked not only the play but the audience, complaining that the "evening-gowned and dinner-jacketed" group was more interested in the "society-girl" actress, Tallulah Bankhead, than it was in any serious social commentary.

Mary the Third (1923)

The Characters--MARY THE FIRST (1870), MARY THE SECOND (1897) and MARY THE THIRD (1923), all played by the same actress, are young women of three generations, each courted by a lover, WILLIAM for Mary the First, ROBERT for Mary the second, LYNN for Mary the Third (William, Robert and Lynn are all played by the same actor); RICHARD: unsuccessful suitor for Mary the Second; GRANNY: Mary the First as grandmother; MOTHER: Mary the Second as mother; FATHER: Mary the Third's father; BOBBY: her younger brother; HAL: Lynn's rival for Mary the Third; LETTIE, MAX and NORA: her friends.

Plot Summary--PROLOGUE: In two scenes Mary the First and Mary the Second are wooed by, respectively, William and Robert. Both Marys are passionate, idealistic, somewhat coquettish, portraying feminine ideals of their generations. They and their suitors are convinced their love is eternal and they will live happily ever after. The parallelism of the two scenes clearly demonstrates that lovers are always convinced that no love in history has ever been as perfect as their own, and are never able to think realistically.

ACT I: Summer, 1922. Mary the First (Granny) is 75 and Mary the Second (Mother) is 46. In direct contrast to the passionate, idealistic optimism of the prologue scenes, Granny and Mother are quarreling idly, both complaining about the younger generation, and about each other. Mary the Third, on entrance, is very much the "new woman," independent, scornful of the past, impatient to lead her own life. Clearly, however, she is more like her mother and her grandmother than she knows: she too is being romanced, she too is unable to decide between Hal and Lynn. She has a modern solution, however: she means to go camping with them--unchaperoned--to determine which is more compatible. She responds scornfully to her mother's objections, saying that her parents' lives would have been happier if they had experimented more before marrying.

ACT II, Scene 1. In a speeding car. Mary, Lettie, Hal, Max and Lynn are off on their adventure. Mary and Lynn are reckless, speeding excitedly into the unknown; cautious Hal seems concerned and fearful.

ACT II, Scene 2. Very early the next morning, back at the family home. Hal, Lynn, Letty and Max creep in through a window; Lynn is carrying Mary, who now confesses that she faked appendicitis to end the camping trip. The others are disgruntled since she had planned the trip to begin with. Mary has been having second thoughts about the whole excursion, rejecting any solution which involves sneaky behavior. The young people discuss marriage, divorce, "being modern." Mary is adamant; whatever they choose to do, they must be honest.

Bobby warns Mary that Dad is furious because of the camping trip. Bobby finds her "a queer nut" for getting herself into trouble; she explains that she is tired of conformity. She is amusing in her condescension to her parents, sure she knows much more about Life than anyone their age does.

Enter Mother and Father, who discuss their problem children without knowing that both of them are hiding, listening. Father suspects the worst: "She's bolted." Mother demurs. They quarrel, wondering if their marriage has been worth what they put into it. When Mother wonders if they would have married each other, knowing how things would turn out, neither can answer. When they leave the stage, still searching for Mary, she comes out from behind the curtain, stricken because her parents hate each other. The scene ends with accusations and counter-accusations across the generations; parents and children all feel betrayed.

ACT III. A cold scene. Father hides behind the newspaper, Mother forces herself to speak--stiffly. Enter Granny, who rattles on cheerfully about how a man should be petted and made much of in the morning, until he is comfortable and relaxed. When Mary enters, the atmosphere becomes even chillier. Mary demands that her parents divorce if they don't love each other; her father shouts that this is romantic nonsense and stalks out. Although passionately sincere Mary sounds a bit naive, assuming that her generation will solve all the problems that her mother and grandmother, whose marriages were "on a *very low* plane," could not. She unintentionally hurts her mother, despite her love for her. The discussion continues even more rancorously when Father and the young people return, amid much discussion of the nature of marriage. When Mother says she's going to leave for a time, to sort herself out, Father follows her. When Mary asks if he loves her mother, he only tells her that she has much to learn about love and marriage.

After all of this Lynn still loves Mary and begs her to marry him. They discuss the pitfalls of marriage, and when Lynn calls her an angel she begs him not to, suspecting that her grandfather had also called her grandmother an angel, and knelt at her feet. (He did.) And so Mary the Third and her lover make the same promises, and the same mistakes, with the same passionate enthusiasm as Mary the First and Mary the Second--all the while convinced such love as theirs has never been seen before. The play ends with their kiss.

Critical Overview--*Mary the Third* opened at the 39th Street Theatre (NY) on 5 February 1923, produced by Lee Shubert in association with Mary Kirkpatrick. Chosen as one of Burns Mantle's Best Plays of 1923, it played 160 performances (P16.1). Critical reception was mixed, since the play's attack on marriage made some of the critics uneasy, but all the reviewers considered it deserving of serious attention whether they liked it or not.

The *New York Times* (R178) called it pretentious in its philosophic content, but added that it was one of the best plays Crothers had written. The review criticized the breadth of Crothers's attack on "marriage and nearly everything connected with it," however, saying the play was weakened by insisting too strenuously on its theme.

Ruth Crosby Dimmick in the *New York Telegraph* (R173) was more enthusiastic: "Every now and then Rachel Crothers comes near hitting the bulls-eye with one of her considerable variety of plays, and last evening [she] came close enough to win commendation from a first night crowd." The *New York Globe* (R175) called it Crothers's most worthwhile play to date, despite its considerable faults. The reviewer praised the plot but criticized the dialogue as "only intermittently natural." While most critics praised the acting, especially of Louise Huff, this reviewer found her "forced."

The *New York Telegram* (R181) praised the play's "delightful quaintness" and wholesomeness, but the *World* (R171) declared that the play revealed nothing about modern marriage, and failed to live up to a promising beginning. Charles Darnton (R172) liked the acting but disliked Mary's idea of trial marriage and the happy, "love conquers all" ending. The *Brooklyn Times* (R183) was positively waspish in tone: "The institution of marriage came in for a lot of pretty hard knocks at the hands of Rachel Crothers" in the play, the review complained. "Perhaps Miss Crothers [is attempting] to justify the fact that she managed to retain the prefix of 'Miss' to her name." Despite this personal comment, the rest of the review was entirely positive.

Theatre Magazine (R177) was also rather negative and condescending, calling the play "another theatre-piece" which glorifies the younger generation and is "spirited in its picture of youthful idealism against the horrors of that somber old institution, marriage." The review laughs at Crothers for discovering Free Love, then getting "very excited about it." It is unimpressed by the play's "daring young heroine that would have been spanked in 1907 but is more or less to be pitied today." The review concludes that this heroine is "quite contemptible" in her "insistence on [her parents] leaving each other forthwith." Ruth Snyder in The *Journal* (I182) took both Crothers and the play more seriously, however, printing an extensive interview on the subject of Crothers's opinion of the modern generation and emphasizing her psychological and emotional honesty in the play.

One interesting sidelight can be noted: The play's original casting included Humphrey Bogart. He apparently became ill while the play was still trying out in Connecticut, however, for, although his face can be seen in one of the publicity photos, his name is not included in the New York cast. Background information on cast members mentions John Alexander, who took over a role when the actor who was to play it--presumably Bogart--became ill in New Haven.

Expressing Willie (1924)

The Characters--MINNIE WHITCOMB: a drab, submissive, self-effacing but still appealing spinster from the small town of Tuckerville; WILLIE SMITH: a Tuckerville boy who has made good in the big city; MRS. SMITH: his mother, still very much from Tuckerville and dubious of citified sophistication and opulence; TALIAFERRO: a witty, urbane man of the world, difficult to impress but charming underneath his aloof exterior; GEORGE and DOLLY CADWALADER--super-sophisticates like Taliaferro, but equally good-hearted under their mockery; FRANCES SYLVESTER: an intense, self-dramatizing woman, in love with Willie and much given to gushing contemporary psychological cliches; SIMPSON, REYNOLDS, JEAN and GORDON: the Smiths' servants.

Plot Summary--ACT I. The setting throughout the play is Willie's "ridiculously magnificent" Italianate mansion on Long Island, shrieking his nouveau riche status as a successful inventor and salesman. Much of the satire comes from the exaggerated, glittering wealth of the setting, contrasting especially to the down-to-earth quality of Minnie Whitcomb and Willie's mother.

As the play begins the audience sees that Willie's mother, suspicious of Willie's wealthy new friends, has invited Minnie, his mousey former girlfriend from Tuckerville, to visit. The farcical tone is established from the beginning: Willie doesn't know Minnie was invited, she thinks he asked her, and she has no idea that fashionable guests will also be present. Mrs. Smith, tart-tongued and honest, fully intends to shake Willie out of his complacency, re-establish down-home values and see to it that he doesn't marry the affected Frances.

When Taliaferro and the Cadwaladers arrive Minnie is awkward and embarrassed, overwhelmed by her lack of sophistication. Together they await Frances, who clearly intends to capture Willie; she raves about the house, the decor, about everything. Minnie's distress reaches a peak when, having reluctantly agreed to play the piano, she falls flat on her face crossing the floor. She withdraws in tears of embarrassment, to be told by Willie that it's probably just as well she fell down before reaching the piano, since his guests are only interested in the very best of art.

ACT II, Scene 1. Later the same evening. The party is still swinging; the guests speak patronizingly of Minnie, feeling sorry for her. Suddenly, however, Minnie reappears, looking strangely luminous. She sits down at the piano and plays with inspiration and courage which mount as the power and beauty of the music grow. She finishes in an extravagant crescendo. Frances doesn't like losing the limelight, but everyone else is stunned. Amidst some comic development of the contemporary fad for self-expression instead of self-effacement Minnie explains that she is a changed woman who wants to be free, however briefly. Willie is clearly nonplussed by this new Minnie.

ACT II, Scene 2. Willie's bedroom. Much to Willie's dismay Minnie appears, "wearing a very wholesome blue dressing gown." He tries to tell her that bedroom conversations are not discreet; she is filled with energy and a compulsion to be truthful and free. She explains that after her embarrassment at falling down, she had prayed for some power to save her--and it did. Suddenly a voice from deep inside spoke to her and told her the truth, that she had been a coward all her life, afraid to live and afraid to give her love. She insists that it was her fault that Willie has grown tired of her.

Suddenly there is a knock on the door. Willie frantically hides her in a closet and opens the door to admit a Frances equally intent upon self-revelation. When Minnie is revealed Frances is enraged, vowing to leave as early as possible the next morning. She sweeps out and the scene ends with Minnie exhorting Willie to find the greatness in himself, shaking him vigorously in a comic effort to help him shake that greatness out.

ACT III. Early the next morning, Minnie is trying to convince Frances that nothing happened, but comic interruptions intervene; the Cadwaladers sweep in and out, smelling scandal and getting everything wrong. There is much rushing about and many comic misunderstandings. Amidst comic business about the need for self-expression, nobody listens to anything anyone else says. Finally, after much frustration and misunderstanding, Minnie and Willie realize they have always loved each other, although his success and her low self-esteem had gotten in the way. Willie realizes he has been a self-centered fool; Minnie that she has failed to assert herself. Encouraged by Taliaferro she hopes to pursue her music, and Willie supports her in this choice, although he also wants to claim her love again. This will be more difficult, however, as the comic ending illustrates; ironically, Minnie is so overjoyed at having found herself and her own creativity that she is no longer especially interested in Willie. Perhaps love will rule later; right now, self-expression does.

Critical Overview--*Expressing Willie* opened 16 April 1924 at the Forty-eighth Street Theatre (NY), to enthusiastic reviews. It was produced by the Equity Players and staged and directed by Crothers. It played 281 performances (P17.1).

John Corbin of the *New York Times* (R185), Heywood Broun of the *New York World* (R184) and Alexander Woollcott of the *New York Sun* (R190) joined in praising the Equity Players for finally finding "one entirely satisfactory thing," as Woollcott put it, in an otherwise "floundering" season. *Theatre Magazine* (R186) agreed, calling the group "unlucky" in their previous endeavors and praising them for producing this play, marked by "clever and hilarious situations, unusually witty dialogue," excellent acting and wonderful stage direction. Corbin called the audience enthusiasm unprecedented, adding that "few could have anticipated the perfect conjunction of play-writing, acting and stage management" even from so skilled a hand as Crothers's. Broun especially praised the subtlety of the satire, remarking that Crothers "realizes that satire does not mean knocking a person down and digging your heels in his face," and that she produced a "sensitive and compelling portrait" of contemporary attitudes. All the critics praised the variety of Crothers's skills as author and director.

A Lady's Virtue (1925)

The Characters--HARRY HALSTEAD: a successful, prosperous young man more interested in his hobby of flying airplanes than in his marriage; SALLY HALSTEAD: his wife, as bored with marriage as Harry; MADAME SISSON: a French singer with a weakness for airplanes and airplane pilots; MONTIE: a young socialite who has been wooing Sally for some time; Mr. and Mrs. WALTER LUCAS: friends of the Halsteads'; RALPH LUCAS: their son; EUGENIO and TSHSTANOFF: Sally's New York acquaintances.

Plot Summary--ACT I. The living room in the Lucas home, in a small American city. Married for eight years, Sally is bored and restless, challenged by her New York friends to do something more interesting and unconventional than remaining married to a man who is clearly more interested in being a pilot than in being a husband. Both Sally and Harry are superficial, selfish people with more money and less responsibility than is good for them; Sally especially is much given to large statements about principles like honesty and freedom of which she has little apparent knowledge.

ACT II. Sally has made the acquaintance of Madame Sisson, an exotic and sophisticated French singer who seems to be her exact opposite. Fascinated by Sisson, Sally insists that she come home with her; when she does, the singer and Harry immediately hit it off. Sally is overjoyed at this test of her liberal principles; she wishes them the best, advises them to pursue their feeling wherever it takes them, and leaves for New York, where she intends to find Montie and perhaps take him up on his frequent professions of love for her.

ACT III, Scene 1. Montie's apartment in New York. When Sally begins to know the real Montie she discovers, not only that he has no intention of being faithful to her (the telephone directory seems to be his favorite reading material), but that, in his self-absorption, he is as boring as Harry. She also realizes that Montie has no intention of marrying her, or perhaps anyone. Disillusioned at his clumsy propositions she leaves his apartment, hoping to find Harry at Sisson's apartment.

ACT III, Scene 2. Madame Sisson's apartment in New York. Sally rushes in to discover that Harry, too, had already begun to reconsider his disillusionment with marriage. Sisson, although she had planned to marry Harry, is unexpectedly honest and generous in giving him up, declaring that the marriage bond is sacred after all. Sally and Harry return home, apparently convinced that their marriage, even if it isn't perfect, is well worth saving.

Critical Overview--*A Lady's Virtue* opened 23 November 1925 at the Bijou Theatre (NY), produced by the Shuberts and staged by Crothers, with settings by Watson Barrett. It played 136 performances (P18.1).

The critics were generally pleased by *A Lady's Virtue*, finding it witty and sophisticated if somewhat superficial. The *New York Times* (R193) praised the characterization, the comic style and the skillful structure, but found it ultimately unsatisfying in its conventionality. "Miss Crothers seems to have clipped her wings with the shears of a dogmatic purpose," the review concluded, hoping for "more daring flights" in future plays. The *Times* was enthusiastic about the Nash sisters in the lead roles, however, mentioning the enthusiastic audience response.

The reviewer in *Theatre Magazine* (R194) praised Crothers's "unerring" theatrical instinct which enabled her to consistently provide an entertaining, diverting evening to a pleased audience even in a play which was found to be occasionally melodramatic and sentimental. Stephen Rathbun of the *New York Sun* (R195) agreed, finding that the play, while somewhat formulaic and conventional, was an audience-pleaser and was sure to be a hit. Like other reviewers, he praised the acting of the Nash sisters.

Percy Hammond in the *New York Herald Tribune* (R192) was less pleased by the play, finding it only mediocre fare. While praising some of the scenes, notably the one between Sally and Montie in his apartment, he found the play ultimately "implausible." Alan Dale in the *New York American* (R191) was also reserved in his approval, finding the play "a bit missionary" in its insistence that "men are really not quite nice" and that women should share in men's freedom. Dale did, however, judge the play to be amusing, ingenious and unpretentious.

Venus (1927)

The Characters--VIRGIE GIBBS:a mature, intelligent woman, hostess of a gathering which is the setting of the play; DR. DICKIE WAKELY: a scientist whose experiment with an amazing new drug starts the principal action of the plot; HERBERT and AGNES BEVERIDGE: guests at Virgie's party; DIANA GIBBS and ROSS HURST: young aviators just returned from a flight to Venus and bubbling over with the wonders of the advanced civilization there; also guests at Virgie's party; MASON: a servant.

ACT I. At Virgie's apartment in Manhattan, on a rooftop terrace. The scene opens with a babble of excited chatter about the completion of the pioneer space flight to Venus, and the return of the first travelers there. A backdrop of 50-story buildings with aircraft landing stations on their top floors, suggestions of spacecraft hovering about in the background and other futuristic details establishes the fantasy element in the play.

In the midst of all the space-chatter Dr. Wakefield announces that he has perfected the entirely appropriate drug for the new age--a potion guaranteed to minimize sex differences by accentuating gentle, feminine qualities in males and strong, masculine qualities in females. He volunteers to use the present party-guests in an experiment, and they excitedly agree.

ACT II. In Virgie's living room. The disastrous results of the experiment suggest that Dr. Wakefield misjudged the correct dosage of his wonder drug. Instead of smoothing out the differences between the sexes and leaving everyone in a kind of happy androgynous middle ground, his potion has simply reversed and intensified role behavior. The gentle Agnes swills Scotch, roars, blusters and bosses people around; Hubert minces, simpers, and flirts outrageously over a Spanish shawl. Only Diana and Ross, the young aviators, still have any balance at all, since they had been at a harmoniously androgynous level to begin with.

ACT III. The inappropriate sex-linked behavior climaxes when Herbert does a colossally clumsy fandango, then subsides in tears, hurt by Agnes's rudeness. Gradually the effects of the drug wear off, and the Beveridges begin to realize what has happened. Finally free of the drug's effects, they retreat happily into their traditional roles, entirely reconciled to a marriage whose strictures they had earlier questioned. Wife loves husband, husband loves wife, and Virgie, seeing all this bliss, accepts Dr. Wakefield's offer of marriage. Diana and Ross, however, still yearning for the advanced state of spiritual and intellectual evolution they had seen on Venus, decide to return to that paradise, leaving Earth's sexual role-playing and hostilities behind.

Critical Overview--Venus opened 26 December 1927 at the Masque Theatre (NY), produced by Carl Reed and staged by Crothers. The futuristic settings were done by Livingston Platt. It played 8 performances (P19.1).

Critical response to Venus was nothing short of savage, with several critics offering their sympathy to the actors caught in the disaster. The tone of the reviews was disgusted at worst, heavy-handedly condescending at best, and unanimous in condemnation.

Alison Smith of the New York World (R199) managed to find a word of praise for Crothers's earlier successes before condemning Venus as a "crazy-quilt" of "cock-eyed" delirium so disorganized as to baffle any attempt at classification or judgment. She found the spectacle of switched gender behavior embarrassing rather than amusing and ended with the sarcastic reflection that she never dreamed she'd see the day when the "mixed ethics but clear exposition of '39 East' seemed by comparison a pleasure to watch and write about."

Richard Watts in the New York Herald Tribune (R200) sneered that Crothers should probably be forgiven for the mess that was Venus, since she had probably so exhausted herself inventing the bizarre details of the plot that she had no energy left over for making sense of them. Calling the play "inept and sophomoric" the review pronounced it one of the season's worst ventures.

Only Brooks Atkinson of the New York Times (R197) made even an attempt at a positive judgment, calling the play's theme "uncommonly imaginative" but finding the play itself a failure, with Crothers missing opportunities to develop the idealism and vision latent in her material. Atkinson expressed sympathy for Tyrone Power in the role of Herbert Beveridge; Powers's wife had died only days before the play's opening, and Atkinson commented that he played his role "willingly and well," although he must have found its silliness exceptionally unpleasant under the circumstances.

Let Us Be Gay (1929)

The Characters--KITTY BROWN: an idealistic young wife who, when her illusions are shattered, becomes a somewhat cynical divorcee; BOB BROWN:

her husband; MRS. BOUCICAULT: a grande dame whose weekend invitation unintentionally reunites the unwitting Bob and Kitty; DIERDRE LESSING: Mrs. Boucicault's rebellious 20-year-old granddaughter, intent on throwing herself away on an older man--Bob Brown; MADGE LIVINGSTON: a vain, self-promoting woman who makes conquests of all the available men, especially Wallace Grainger; BRUCE KEEN: Dierdre's beau, with whom she has become bored; TOWNLEY TOWN and WALLACE GRAINGER: socialite weekend guests who both fall more or less in love with Kitty; STRUTHERS, WILLIAMS and PERKINS: servants at Mrs. Boucicault's country place.

Plot Summary--PROLOGUE: In Kitty's charming, feminine bedroom. Kitty, distraught, is weeping as Bob, unseen, pounds on her door; she refuses to let him in. She is ending their marriage because he has been unfaithful. He insists it meant nothing, but she refuses to be consoled. Her marriage had meant everything to her; if Bob could take it so lightly there is nothing left for her.

ACT I. A few years later, at Mrs. Boucicault's place in Westchester, a luxurious establishment worthy of Noel Coward. Mrs. Boucicault has invited an intriguing mystery lady to provide competition for Dierdre, her daring granddaughter who is engaged to Bruce but flirting desperately and successfully with Bob Brown. The mystery lady turns out to be Kitty, but she and Bob have not seen each other yet. She knows she's supposed to distract someone, and there's comic byplay as she flirts successfully with, in succession, Townley, Bruce and Wallace, who is very much Madge's property.

Madge is a comic caricature, whining, demanding, attracting great attention to herself with endless requests for glasses of water, fetched handkerchiefs, furniture to be moved for her greater comfort and to show her off more attractively.

When Kitty and Bob meet, both are stunned but keep their composure. Kitty explains that she's using her maiden name, Courtland, to keep her individuality and avoid having to use Bob's name. The comic potential is fully exploited as they exchange comments like "Haven't I met you before," without giving the game away to the other members of the group.

Everybody flirts with everybody; all the men, to Madge's disgust, are fascinated by the dangerously charming Kitty. As they discuss romance and marriage Kitty reveals herself as much more cynical, witty and disillusioned than she had appeared in the Prologue. The dialogue is brittle, sophisticated and comic. Madge stoutly defends marriage as the most sacred thing in the world, an effect only slightly spoiled by Wallace, her attentive swain to whom she is definitely not married. Madge is appalled, however, when Wallace wins the honor of Kitty's company on a walk.

ACT II, Scene 1. Two hours later. More flirtatious badinage as Madge upbraids the faithless Wallace, who defends himself unconvincingly. Madge criticizes the shocking younger generation, but Mrs. Boucicault says she prefers Dierdre's brazenness to Madge's slyness. This comic business is interrupted with a serious scene between Bob and Kitty. Bob is offended by her worldliness; she doesn't care. He is appalled to hear that she is a successful business woman; she praises the experience of making and spending her own money, living as independently as a man.

ACT II, Scene 2. An hour later, on Kitty's balcony. A hilarious, comedy-of-errors scene. First Townley climbs up to chat with Kitty; he vows he loves her, then swears and slaps a mosquito. Just as he kisses her, Bob wanders onto the balcony from his room, which also abuts it. Townley doesn't understand her unexpectedly close relationship with Bob (they still haven't revealed their relationship). Bob certainly doesn't understand what Townley was doing kissing her. Townley leaves; Bob protests; Kitty retorts that what's good for the goose is good for the gander.

Then Dierdre comes up to speak to Kitty; she is appalled to find her in Bob's room. Kitty refuses to protest her innocence because she thinks Dierdre should be disillusioned now, not after marriage. The hypocrisy of the double standard is revealed here; male philandering seems much more acceptable than female flirtation.

ACT III. Nine a.m. the following day. Bruce pursues Dierdre, who is disillusioned and angry and pushes everyone away. The comedy continues to develop as Dierdre complains about Kitty, revealing that she found Kitty in Bob's room; Bruce wonders what she was doing there herself. As they quarrel they examine the double standard; Bruce defends the idea of perfect, untouched womanhood, but Dierdre wonders "where the hell" a girl is to find a man equally pure. Finally Bob stuns the group by revealing that he and Kitty were once married. Kitty regrets having started the whole discussion, since it is clear that everyone is only too willing to believe the worst about her.

Good-byes begin as the country weekend begins to break up. Finally Kitty and Bob share the stage alone; he wants to start again. She says there's nothing left. He pleads for a chance to make her love him again. She protests that love isn't enough. Finally, however, she mentions how lonely she is. He embraces her; she declares her undiminished love and asks him to take her back. The curtain falls as they kiss.

Critical Overview--*Let Us Be Gay* opened on 21 February 1929, at the Little Theatre (NY). It was produced by John Golden and directed by Crothers. Selected by Burns Mantle as one of the Best Plays of 1930-31, it played 132 performances (P20.1). It was made into a film in 1930.

Gilbert Gabriel (R203) described it as a pleasant social comedy in which the characters gathered at an unusually interesting house party are faithfully and revealingly dissected, providing both entertainment and acute social observation. He also praised the sense of purpose common to Crothers's works, in which one can always find development of interesting and relevant moral points, subtly and effectively done.

Brooks Atkinson in the *New York Times* (R201) called Crothers a "gallant playwright with an active, sunny mind," and especially praised the effectiveness of her direction.

Percy Hammond in the *New York Herald Tribune* (R204) called "Miss Rachel Crothers's house party...one of the more amusing festivals of its kind, permitting those who like to on-look and eavesdrop at such functions an excellent opportunity to be entertained." The play is "one of those smart comedies wherein woman's wear is called a 'frock', and there is tea upon the terrace, water sports in the swimming pool, trysts upon the balcony overlooking the rosegarden."

St. John Ervine, in the *New York World* (R202), praised the vigorous dialogue. The *Daily News* said the audience took the advice of the title, and had fun which was grammatical, sophisticated and much appreciated.

Robert Littell, in *Theatre Arts Monthly* (R205), praised the author's competent direction and called *Let Us Be Gay* one of the best recent American social comedies. He liked the "sparkle," "surface smartness and civilized irresponsibility" which Crothers maintained without degenerating into farce. He was also enthusiastic about the "author's very positive convictions about love and marriage."

Arthur Pollock of the *Brooklyn Eagle* (R207) praised the smart, sophisticated tone of the play, proclaiming it a "lucky week for the theater" when *Let Us Be Gay* opened. Gabriel Gilbert of the New York American (R203) was especially pleased by the lighthearted comedy of this play, coming as it did so soon after *Venus*, "that strange, wretched fantasy...which blighted Christmas night a season ago." He proclaimed that Crothers has "redeemed herself" with this new effort. Only Mark Van Doren, in *The Nation* (R208), was somewhat reserved in his praise. He predicted inevitable success for the play, calling it clever and intelligent, but warned that Crothers was becoming somewhat formulaic and conventional in her productions.

On tour, the play opened in Los Angeles on 2 March 1930. Critics were enthusiastic, calling it a delightful comedy of manners and a revealing, perceptive social commentary. Both the lighthearted tone and of the writing and the excellent quality of the production were praised by the critics.

The play was also revived in Baltimore in June 1943, starring Gloria Swanson.

The 1930 film, which starred Norma Shearer as Kitty, Marie Dressler as Mrs. Boucicault and Hedda Hopper as Madge Livingston, was directed by Robert Z. Leonard. It received very favorable reviews, especially in the Los Angeles papers, where Louella Parsons pronounced it a delight.

As Husbands Go (1931)

The Characters--LUCILE LINGARD: a vibrant, beautiful woman of 35 who is traveling in Europe and finds Paris more fascinating than Dubuque, a young English poet more fascinating than her staunch, patient husband at home; RONALD DERBYSHIRE: the poet in question, in love with Lucile but primarily interested in himself; EMMIE SYKES: Lucile's friend and traveling companion, a comic and slightly dizzy widow of 45 who is determined to create an exciting new life for herself; HIPPOLITUS LOMI: the very sophisticated European gentleman of 60 with whom she means to share that exciting life-- along with her money; MAITRE D'HOTEL and WAITER: employees at the restaurant where this foursome dines; CHARLES LINGARD: Lucile's adoring, entirely four-square American husband who likes Dubuque as much as she likes

Paris; WILBUR: Charles's young nephew; PEGGY SYKES: Emmie's daughter, who disapproves of her mother's frivolity; JAKE CANON: her laconic, straight-shooting boyfriend, a Gary Cooper type; CHRISTINE and KATIE: servants.

Plot Summary--PROLOGUE: a chic cafe in Paris, 4 a.m. Lucile and Emmie are both wearing French evening gowns and looking extremely smart. The evening is replete with champagne, dancing and romance. The women dread returning to Dubuque after the glories of Paris; the gentlemen are equally reluctant to see them leave. Ronald woos Lucile, who is torn by her real love for the faithful Charles at home and her desire for the more dashing and exciting Ronald. Emmie worries that Lucile is making a mistake; Lucile worries that Emmie has fallen for a fortune-hunter. They discuss the difference between Parisian sophistication and Iowan simplicity comically and at length, passionately phrasing their desire to live, at least briefly, for themselves instead of for husband, children or convention. Finally Lucile decides that she will leave Charles when she gets home.

ACT I: The comfortable living room in country home near Dubuque. No style, but pleasant. Charles is lovingly checking the flowers he has gathered for Lucile's return. Enter Lucile, beautiful but nervous. Charles covers her with kisses. As the characters gradually assemble a comedy of errors develops: Emmie's daughter Peggy is horrified by Hippie, who has come with them from Europe, and Emmie in return is horrified by Jake, Peggy's fiance.

Before the act ends Emmie reproaches Lucile for not telling Charles the truth about Ronald. Lucile reproaches Emmie for having mentioned him to begin with. At the very end Charles springs his real surprise--he has asked his nephew Wilbur to live with them, sure that Lucile would sympathize with the boy's lack of other family. Not surprisingly, she lacks the courage to tell him about Ronnie on top of that.

ACT II, Scene 1: Later the same week, early evening. The comic misunderstandings of the previous act continue. Lucile permits everyone to think that Ronald, who has suddenly shown up in the middle of Iowa, is pursuing Emmie; Peggy is even more horrified by this possibility than she was by Hippie. Different cultures and different generations--European and American, young and old--debate love, conformity, fidelity and self-fulfillment. Charles begins to realize that Lucile is not entirely happy in Dubuque; he thinks perhaps she wants a singing career, but fears that she wants more than that. He and Ronald arrange to go fishing early the next morning, but Charles knows something is wrong and suspects that Ronald might be a part of it.

ACT II, Scene 2: The next day. The two mighty fishermen come in, tired, chilled to the bone, but sated with the joys of a successful fishing expedition. They exchange compliments about fishing prowess, being "a man's man," and the like; they also share more than a few drinks, and it becomes apparent that Charles wants to get Ronald drunk. They discuss morality, women, the differences between Europe and America. Ronald, who has agreed to take Lucile dancing that night because Charles doesn't dance, is becoming a little hazy on the time of the appointment; Charles suggests that it was probably the night before. Charles wonders if he has hampered Lucile's chance at a singing career; Ronald doesn't think she has the talent or stamina for such an endeavor. Ronald also reveals his essential selfishness, asserting that he wants a woman to take care of him. He claims a spark of genius which must come first, before any woman. Women come and go, he adds comfortably, but his genius will remain. Just before the curtain Lucile comes onstage, realizes that both the men in her life are drunk, and lashes out: "You're beasts!--Disgusting--loathsome *beasts!*" When Ronald innocently apologizes for missing "the party last night," she stalks off. Charles seems pleased.

ACT III: Noon the next day. Peggy quarrels with Emmie, blaming her for Lucile's peculiar behavior and criticizing her for not acting her age. Emmie responds with wounded dignity, then weeps; when Hippie defends Emmie Peggy attacks him too, then walks off. Emmie is defeated; she tells Hippie it's not worth what she would have to endure from Peggy for the rest of her life if they were to marry. Hippie reveals himself as a thoroughly decent man, not the fortune-hunter he had seemed, accepting Emmie's refusal with real grief. Peggy, ashamed, relents and apologizes; she realizes she'd been selfish and thoughtless, relegating her mother to old age at 45. Emmie in turn accepts Jake as a future son-in-law.

A maid enters with a letter which reveals that Ronald has left, magnanimously leaving Lucile to Charles, whom he praises as a wonderful man whose love is a miracle of selflessness. Since Charles, who is offstage, still doesn't officially know about the romance, Lucile guiltily resolves to tell him immediately. Emmie forbids it, advising her simply to take up with Charles where they had left off. Lucile turns to Wilbur, asking him with great sincerity if he will live with her and Charles; he accepts tearfully. When Charles enters, announcing a Sunday dinner of chicken, mashed potatoes, ice cream and chocolate sauce, Wilbur's happiness is complete and Lucile seems contented. She sinks against Charles without reservation, asking him to hold her, and the curtain falls on the happy threesome.

Critical Overview--Produced by John Golden and directed by Crothers, *As Husbands Go* opened on 5 March 1931 at the John Golden Theatre (NY). It played 148 performances and was selected by Burns Mantle as one of the Best Plays of 1931 (P21.1).

J. Brooks Atkinson in the *New York Times* (R212 and R213) considered the play on two separate occasions. He praised it warmly, focusing on its "wisdom, serenity, humor and abundant sympathy for ordinary people." He especially praised its "merriment," its "hilarious lines," its ability to present clashing points of view with clearmindedness and real emotion. He also commented on Crothers's ability in casting and directing, as well as her brilliant writing.

The critic for the *World Telegram* (R220) agreed, calling *As Husbands Go* "good news" for the current Broadway season. He called the acting "pretty near perfection," adding that the play was "clean without being too clean, adult without being too adult." He, like Atkinson, praised the play's humor, humanity and sense of proportion. Walter Winchell of the *New York Daily Mirror* (R232) was especially pleased by the intelligence of the play, and the simple, brilliant perfection of its comedy.

John Mason Brown, in the *New York Evening Post* (R215), was equally positive: "The aspect of things theatrical, which has not been particularly cheerful of late, brightened up considerably last evening when a merry comedy of Rachel Crothers's fashioning took possession of both the stage and the audience." Crothers's ability as director was also praised. Brown, however, did complain about "technical inadequacies," including clumsy structure and occasional sentimentality. Robert Garland (R221) called the play good news for Broadway, praising Crothers, her producer, and even the "eighteen-karat" audience which fully appreciated this witty, delightful comedy.

Arthur Ruhl of the *Herald* (R229) called the play "first-class entertainment, made out of sound American stuff," the kind of comedy that leaves a "good taste in the mouth." "The audience listened with very evident pleasure and frequently interrupted the players with little spontaneous bursts of applause." Several reviews, including that in the *Morning Telegraph* (R217), stressed the length and durability of Crothers's career, which had contributed so many entertaining plays to the Broadway stage. In fact the social significance of a Crothers production was underlined by articles like the one in the *Evening Post* (R228) which commented, not only on the play, but on the distinguished members of the audience who saw a preview benefit production for the Professional Children's School.

Weeks after it opened, the play was still garnering positive comments, with the critic for the *Herald Tribune* (R230) calling it a "candidate for the Pulitzer glories." During an especially hot summer several critics complimented the play's humor for refusing to melt as others had done. An overview article in *The Woman's Journal* (R211) was also lavish in its praise both of *As Husbands Go* and of Crothers herself, finding her "unique" in her stature as woman playwright and director, a real power in the contemporary theater.

The play was also revived on 19 January 1933 in the Forrest Theatre (NY), produced by J.J. Leventhal and O. E. Wee (P21.2). Critical reception was again positive, praising both the play and the quality of the production. The review in the *New York American* (R245) called the play as good as any of the season's new offerings.

The 1934 film of "As Husbands Go" starred Warner Baxter as Charles Lingard, Helen Vinson as Lucile, Catherine Doucet as Emmie Sykes, Warner Oland as Hippolitus Lomi, and G.P. Huntley Jr. as Ronald Darbyshire.

Caught Wet (1931)

The Characters--CLIFFORD VANDERSTYLE: 26, the priggish, self-satisfied scion of a wealthy New York family; JULIA VANDERSTYLE: 19, his shy, uncertain, pretty-without-knowing-it sister, just out of convent school; TOMMY JONES and PETER SMEED: sophisticated young socialites who are somewhat dubious about the potential for a good time in a rainy weekend with the stuffy Vanderstyles; DOLORES WINTHROP: 22, a strikingly beautiful young woman whom Clifford is courting; ELIZABETH BETTS: her daring, independent young friend; MICHAEL MEER: a struggling musician who entertains at parties to make ends meet; he falls in love with Elizabeth; STANLEY: a servant who is really a private detective; BREWSTER and PETERSON: servants; A WATCHMAN: a member of the local police force.

Plot Summary--ACT I. Time: The present. All action takes place in the living room of the Vanderstyles' country house on the Hudson, a handsome room of dated elegance and heavy ornamentation, but also of beauty and obvious wealth. Setting, action and dialogue clearly establish the play as a comedy of manners. The young people have gathered at the Vanderstyles' for a weekend but rain is dampening both their plans and their spirits. Clifford is enamored of Dolores, who is secretly in love with Peter, but considering Clifford because of his wealth and position. The dialogue is smart and brittle; Clifford reveals himself to be pompous and stuffy, while Betty is witty, daring and rather cynical.

Betty requests a cocktail but Clifford considers drinking vulgar during Prohibition, although he boasts of his fine cellar of pre-war liquor. He also requests more prudent conversation and behavior in front of his innocent young sister, Julia. who will be joining them.

Betty, Dolores, Peter and Tommy discuss the Vanderstyles' great wealth, their dislike of Peter's pomposity, and their boredom with the rainy weekend. Finally they hatch a plan: they will steal the Vanderstyles' heirloom pearls just to create a stir, then return them when they've had their fun. Before the act ends Julia is revealed to be a sweet, intelligent but unsophisticated girl; Michael, who was scheduled to provide musical entertainment, also reveals himself as an amateur sleight-of-hand artist.

ACT II: Amidst flirtation and parlor games an attraction between Michael and Betty develops; they are both poor but independent. The dialogue is light and comic, and the byplay to distract Clifford and Julia from the pearls is entertaining. Finally Michael snatches the pearls; just as their loss is realized the lights go out. Pandemonium ensues, since this was not part of the plan. Everyone accuses everyone else and Clifford's essential unpleasantness is revealed, since he even accuses Dolores. Stanley's identity as an undercover cop is revealed and Clifford instructs him to question everyone. As the lights go out again, everything from ghosts to political conspirators is blamed.

ACT III: Much suspicion, much hostility, much "this is enough of the game" but no one knows how to end it. Clifford's pomposity becomes more and more obvious. Dolores becomes less and less convinced that he's worth his money, more and more convinced that she loves Peter, and he loves her. Amidst a great deal of visual comedy even the imperturbable Stanley looks guilty for a moment. The main finger of suspicion points at Michael Meer, since no one knows him and he was a replacement for the original pianist. Betty, too, is under suspicion since the idea was hers and she admits she'd do anything for a dare.

After a great deal of comic confusion and misunderstanding things begin to clear up. Julia is revealed as the real "thief"; she had overheard some of the scheme, and had hidden the pearls herself to prevent a real theft. She asserts her independence, convincing Tommy to run off with her and the pearls, so that she can escape Clifford's domination. The final joke is on Clifford, who is made to look a fool not only in front of his guests, but in front of his servants. Michael and Betty are paired up, as are Dolores and Peter.

Critical Overview--Produced by John Golden and staged by Crothers, *Caught Wet* opened 4 November 1931 at the John Golden Theatre (NY). Almost entirely negatively reviewed, it played only 13 performances (P22.1).

Richard Lockridge of the *New York Sun* (R224) judged that the play was conspicuous in its lack of all those qualities one expects from a Crothers comedy. He complained that the plot was only a "trivial parlor game" played "kittenishly" by a dramatist who obviously knows better and wondered if Crothers was not simply wasting her considerable talent.

Percy Hammond in the *New York Herald-Tribune* (R222) noted that Crothers is usually a conscientious playwright, but that she had "deviated from the paths of her usual credibility" in *Caught Wet*. Like Lockridge he complained about improbability of both characters and behavior.

While Robert Garland of the *World-Telegram* (R221) was kinder than the other critics, praising much of the dialogue as being "as wise, as worldly and as witty as anything the playwright has devised," he too concluded that the play itself went "nowhere in particular."

John Hutchens in *Theatre Arts Monthly* (R239) echoed the harsh judgments of the newspaper critics. He praised Crothers for making an attempt at a satire of bad manners, but concluded that Crothers made a mistake in "asking you first to dislike a set of excessively irksome boys and girls" and then later demanding sympathy for them. He concluded that the play "promised not to work and it didn't."

When Ladies Meet (1932)

The Characters--MARY HOWARD: an attractive, "carelessly chic" woman, a successful novelist who is concerned with woman's roles both in her fiction and in her own life; JIMMIE LEE: her engaging, devil-may-care friend who is at least a little bit in love with her but who insists on criticizing both her fiction and her behavior; MRS. BRIDGET DRAKE: her wealthy, giddy, middle-aged friend who has decided not to let her widowed status interfere with her love life; WALTER MANNERS: Bridget's latest conquest; ROGERS WOODRUFF: Mary's publisher, whom she loves and is loved by although he is married; PIERRE: a servant at Bridget's place in Connecticut; CLAIRE WOODRUFF: Rogers's wife.

Plot Summary--ACT I, Scene 1. A pretty Greenwich Village apartment; treetops are visible outside the window. The curtain opens on Jimmie Lee and Mary Howard, both very likeable, knowledgeable people, surrounded by cigarettes, cocktails, all the trappings of New York sophistication.

As the scene opens Mary and Jimmie are bickering fondly; Jimmie vows his love for her, but she insists he's just too lazy to find the great passion he deserves. He retorts that great passions always blow up, defending liking as the greatest human relationship. It outlasts everything else, he asserts. Jimmie praises her ability with decor, her success as a novelist, then complains that she's too choosy, expecting a man to be exactly the way she wants him, like a room she has decorated. No man alive could live up to her expectations, he warns her.

It becomes clear that Mary is a romantic soul yearning for a grand passion; it also becomes clear that the chief candidate is Rogers Woodruff, who is married, a father of two children, and her publisher. The more she protests her innocence, the more clear her infatuation becomes. Jimmie clearly doesn't like Woodruff much, and suggests that if Woodruff were a good editor he would point out to Mary how artificial her writing has become. By now Mary is defending her innocence, her editor and her writing, and is getting a bit cross. Jimmie insists that her first writing was as real as a crooked tree, full of life because it was about something she knew at first hand.

They go on to debate what a "good woman" does and doesn't do. Jimmie is, to say the least, demanding, insisting that men are conventional and conservative on the subject of decent women. Men want women to stay pure even when they make every effort to persuade them to behave other than decently, he warns, muttering that he himself has persuaded many women to surrender all their love to him, then hated them for it later.

Enter Bridget and Walter, with considerable double-entendre gossip about who is currently seeing whom. Bridget clearly thinks Mary needs a lover, perhaps even Woodruff, though he is married; Mary, shocked, protests that their relationship is entirely professional.

Enter Woodruff, and, when they are alone, they reveal their love for each other. In front of the others, however, they still pretend that their relationship is purely business. Their idealism, the intensity of their love and the entangling nature of their predicament become clear as the scene ends.

ACT I, Scene 2. The same place, later that day. Mary and Rogers have a confrontation. Mary, guilty about Rogers's wife and children, wants to end their relationship; Rogers refuses. Mary can't resist his love as a protection against loneliness. She protests that she has been lonely all her life, even when she was too young to understand what loneliness was. How can her love for Rogers be wrong, she wonders, reasoning that since her life is her own, only she will be hurt by this love. She finally concludes that she can't give him up. The emotional intensity of this moment is shattered by Jimmie's voice from the garden below, calling out that he's shinnying up the tree and muttering about damaged clothes and damaged self-esteem if he falls. He teases them about working so late and embarrasses everyone (except himself), talking about sitting next to Rogers's wife at dinner, and how nice and funny she was. Jimmie is still chattering happily as the scene ends.

ACT II, Scene 1. The scene opens in Bridget's luxurious Connecticut place where Mary, Rogers and Walter are spending the weekend. Much of the dialogue deals with the pitfalls facing modern women; Mary discusses her professional, creative and romantic problems with Rogers, while Bridget discusses her own romantic problems with Walter. Like Mary, Bridget is terrified of loneliness; women are made to be loved, she insists, and the love of children does not suffice. Even when her husband was alive she had been lonely, she says soberly, since he was frequently unfaithful.

The serious mood is broken when Jimmie and Claire enter, with an elaborate story of having gotten lost--what Mary doesn't know is that Claire is Rogers Woodruff's wife. Jimmie wants to make Mary jealous and Claire goes along with the game, knowing nothing about Mary and Rogers.

Claire and Mary talk seriously; Claire likes Mary's novels. Mary appreciates her saying that the female characters are "astonishingly true," since Jimmie has been complaining they're not. There is a good deal of comic business about the "coincidence" involved in everyone's being at Bridget's on this particular weekend. Suddenly a storm breaks and it is decided that Jimmie and Claire will stay the night. Rogers has left (he went to New York to see an author he had been trying to work with, unaware that Jimmie had arranged the appointment to get Rogers out of the way) so Claire will have his room.

ACT II, Scene 2. A cozy scene in Mary's bedroom: Mary, Claire and Bridget exchange confidences about the men in their lives. Claire contends that no man is worth the sacrifice of one's self-respect, in the process revealing that her husband has been frequently unfaithful. Claire suggests that the "other woman" in Mary's novel is unconvincingly generous and fair-minded. Eventually Claire begins to suspect the real situation; then there's a knock on the door and Rogers says "Mary--I got back." Rogers is astounded to see Claire, and gradually Jimmie's little scheme is revealed. In private Mary challenges Rogers to tell Claire the truth; he says only "Not here--not now," looking weak and hypocritical as he does so.

ACT III. The next morning, still at Bridget's country place. There is much rushing about and not a little quarreling. Mary is leaving early, angry at everyone but especially at Jimmie for arranging the deception. Claire and Rogers discuss their situation, and Rogers's real weakness and selfishness are revealed; he insists that he and Mary have been only professional friends, pleading with Claire to ignore what she has seen. Claire refuses; she has forgiven his past infidelities, but now that she has met Mary she can't forgive what he did to Mary as well as to herself. She finally blurts out that she has stopped loving him. Their marriage is over, she insists, and leaves. Bridget, discussing men with Mary, reveals her own suffering: even her husband's death had been less painful than his affairs, she says. Mary finally forgives Jimmie, realizing that he has only revealed Rogers's true character; she cannot forgive herself, however, for being the cause of this final hurt to Claire. She can never forget what she saw, she insists; she will never forget Claire's eyes when she realized the truth about her husband. On this somber note the play ends.

Critical Overview--Produced by John Golden at the Royale Theatre (NY), *When Ladies Meet* opened on 6 October 1932 to extremely favorable reviews (P23.1). It played for 173 performances, returning after a brief tour for a second run of 18 performances. World tours took it to London (R244), Budapest, Berlin and Vienna. It was made into films twice, once in 1933 and again in 1941.

Burns Mantle (R242) declared that "There was rejoicing in the theatre set when Rachel Crothers brought her comedy...to the Royale Theatre in early October. There is always rejoicing at the first definite dramatic hit of a new season, and this particular season had seemed pretty empty up till that time." He added that the public supported the hit with a sold-out run of three months, pleased by Crothers's study "of the human family as it is variously domesticated in America."

Robert Garland of the *World Telegram* (R237) agreed, calling it the first solid success and the "outstanding play" of the season. Commenting on the amazing durability of Crothers's career, he pronounced this her finest play yet. John Mason Brown in the *New York Evening Post* (R235) paid particular and favorable attention to Crothers as director, praising her pacing, her dramatically effective use of pauses, her overall directorial intelligence. He was also struck by the originality and effectiveness of her casting.

Brooks Atkinson of the *New York Times* (R233) praised the play's unusual understanding of women as well as its tone, lighthearted and somber by turns. Like Brown he praised Crothers's abilities as a director. Richard Lockridge of the *New York Sun* (R241) agreed, saying the play was perhaps the finest "of all that long procession of admirable plays" Crothers had written. He especially praised the subtle, complex, compassionate tone of the work.

Other reviewers, including Gilbert Gabriel in the *New York American* (R236), emphasized the quality of the acting. Gabriel found special praise for Spring Byington, whom he found blissfully funny as well as poignant.

While nearly all the critical response was overwhelmingly positive, some reservations were expressed. Joseph Wood Krutch, in *The Nation* (R240), predicted that the play would be a success and praised its professionally smooth structure. He objected to Crothers's conventionality, however, finding the play "almost completely spoiled by its moralizing" tone. He also detected more reliance on platitude than real moral vision in Crothers's recent work. Even he, however, found praise for Spring Byington's acting. A similar accusation of conventionality was expressed by Charles Morgan, reviewing the London production for the *New York Times* (R244). Morgan mentioned Crothers's reliance on formulaic structure, but concluded that his objections would not make much difference, since the play was already as big a hit in London as it had been in New York.

The tour in San Francisco was less successful, however. Kay Johnson, Tom Douglas, Catherine Calhoun Doucet and Catherine Willard starred, but the play ran only a few days, having received largely negative reviews.

The filmed version of 1933 was directed by Harry Beaumont and produced by Metro-Goldwyn-Mayer. Its cast included Ann Harding as Claire, Myrna Loy as Mary, Robert Montgomery as Jimmie Lee and Frank Morgan as Woodruff. The film was reviewed by Mordaunt Hall in the *New York Times* (R238) as intelligent and amusing, but "somewhat long on words and short on action." He praised the acting, however, especially that of Myrna Loy.

The version of 1941 fared less well. Again it featured an all-star cast: Joan Crawford as Mary, Robert Taylor as Jimmy Lee, Herbert Marshall as Woodruff, Greer Garson as Claire and Spring Byington as Bridget. The screenplay was by

S.K. Lauren and Anita Loos, and Robert Z. Leonard directed. As reviewed by Bosley Crowther in the *Times* (R261), however, it was dismissed as a dated, "Hoover-vintage" waste of effort, a film which tries desperately for a few fairly amusing minutes, then "expires painfully and pitifully in a smother of pompous words."

Susan and God (1937)

The Characters--SUSAN TREXEL: an impetuous, enthusiastic woman much given to "causes" of one kind or another; somewhat exasperating but loved by her friends and family; BARRIE TREXEL: her loving but estranged husband, a man with a drinking problem; BLOSSOM TREXEL: their 16-year-old daughter, away at boarding school; IRENE BURROUGHS: Susan's socialite friend, in love with MICHAEL O'HARA although she is not yet divorced from her husband, Tom; CHARLOTTE MARLEY: Susan's friend; LEONORA STUBBS: another friend, more or less in love with CLYDE ROCHESTER although she is still married to HUTCHINS STUBBS ("Stubbie"); LEEDS and LEONTINE: servants.

Plot Summary--ACT I, Scene 1. The terrace room in Irene's country home, a fashionable atmosphere appropriate for a Noel Coward play. The opening conversation is equally sophisticated; Irene, Mike, Stubbie, Leonora, Clyde and Charlotte gossip about affairs, divorce, about who's sleeping with whom. It becomes clear that Irene and Mike are having an affair which Irene wants kept secret from Susan when she returns from her stay in England. Susan's marriage to Barrie is also discussed; they all agree that she should divorce him, charming though he is.

When Susan enters, prattling on about having discovered God in an entirely new way and interrupting herself to tell Irene about the "ravishing panties" she has brought for her, she is seen as a gushing enthusiast, a woman more given to whims than to serious concerns.

Audience sympathies are pulled in several directions as the first act ends. Barrie, who enters with Blossom, seems weak but genuinely loving; Blossom, an awkward teenager who sobs that she'd like a traditional family this summer, like everyone else has, is pathetic. Susan, however funny and charming she might be, has obviously not succeeded in providing a home for husband and daughter.

ACT I, Scene 2. Again the group is discussing Susan, who is going around preaching to everyone and making a nuisance of herself. Susan is behaving awkwardly in this sophisticated world by insisting on being absolutely honest, and nobody's very happy about it. Prompted by Susan, Leonora and Clyde admit that they're in love; not too surprisingly, husband Stubbie is not pleased by the revelation. He sulkily asks Susan to leave things alone; Charlotte agrees.

Comedy dominates as Susan rushes around oblivious to everyone's discomfort as well as to the fact that her family situation, too, could be improved. Finally Mike decides to distract her with a fake confession. The scene is comically effective, as Mike searches his soul while Susan innocently encourages him to ask God for help in trying to make himself over. When Barrie overhears and decides to do some reforming of his own the comic misunderstandings increase, since Susan didn't have herself in mind when she talked of change. The scene ends with a slightly-drunk but charming Barrie telling Susan she looks like an angel, and Susan realizing with dismay that she may have started more than she intended.

ACT II, Scene 1. A guest room in Irene's house. Barrie requests a family reconciliation for Blossom's sake. He is humble and apologetic, admitting that most of their troubles were caused by his drinking, but he promises that he can and will change. Susan refuses, until finally Barrie suggests a bargain: if Susan will open their house for the summer, and have Blossom and him living with her, the first time he slips back into drinking he will give her the divorce she wants. Susan agrees reluctantly.

ACT II, Scene 2. The terrace again. The conversation is leisurely Sunday morning gossip with everyone cautious, polite and diffident. When Susan ecstatically informs them all that she, Barrie and Blossom are going to spend the summer together, her friends are more horrified than enthusiastic. Susan's ambivalence is clear; as she tells Irene how much Barrie and Blossom love each other, she blurts out that they will hang on her neck all summer and choke her to death. As the scene comes to an end she wails "I wish I'd never *heard* of God."

ACT III, Scene 1. A lovely room in Susan's home, radiating the comfort and style which are her trademarks. The scene opens on Susan and Irene, who discuss the problems of attempted moral reform; Susan is stifled by her family and Irene is bored and unhappy without Mike. While Susan knows she's being selfish she resents Blossom's friends, who wear her clothes, steal her writing paper and drop in at all hours of the day and night. When Blossom enters, however, it is clear that she thrives on all this domesticity.

A crisis arises when Susan announces her plans to attend a religious revival in Newport. Barrie objects that it's too much time taken from Blossom's last days at home before school. He rejects the idea that she has any message to take to anyone, insisting that "her job" is to make Blossom and him happy. They quarrel, as Susan desperately insists on her right to a life of her own. Barrie accuses her of faking her religious conviction, saying soberly that he doubts she knows anything at all about God. He then stalks off, quite possibly to get drunk.

Act III, Scene 2. In Susan's house. Barrie and Charlotte have disappeared, and there are hints that they might have run off together. Susan is under attack, with Irene insisting that this is what she deserves for meddling in everyone else's affairs (Mike didn't wait for her to take him back, and is marrying someone else.) When Charlotte enters she and Susan quarrel, with Charlotte insisting that she loves Barrie but would have nothing to do with him while he and Susan are together. Susan is impressed against her will, acknowledging Charlotte's loyalty and capacity for self-sacrifice. She praises Charlotte for sticking to Barrie, blaming herself for his return to drinking: "You slipped because I failed you." Barrie insists he alone is to blame for his drinking. Finally Susan, having determined that Barrie is not in love with Charlotte, tells him that she has been wrong. They should stay together, to keep Blossom happy and Barrie sober. As the play ends Susan says, through her tears, that God is not something or someone far away, to be prayed to from a distance. God is inside, in everyone, and he will help only after we have searched inside to find our own sins and shortcomings, she insists. Begging Barrie to hold her, and God not to fail her, Susan embraces Barrie as the play ends.

Critical Overview--*Susan and God* opened 7 October 1937 at the Plymouth Theatre (NY) to mixed but generally enthusiastic reviews. It was produced by John Golden and staged by Crothers, with settings by Jo Mielziner. It played 288 performances and was chosen one of the Best Plays of 1937-38 by Burns Mantle (24.1). It also won the Gold Medal of the Theater Group as the outstanding American play of the season. It toured extensively. Gertrude Lawrence, who created the role in 1937, also starred in a revival at the City Center of Music and Drama in December 1943. It was also made into a film in July 1940.

Writing for the *New York Sun* ((R253), Richard Lockridge was somewhat reserved in his judgement, praising Crothers as a craftsman but adding that the play was somewhat confused. Gertrude Lawrence, however, "all animation and high jinks," won his unqualified praise for a performance which made the audience forget that the plot didn't necessarily make sense.

Richard Watts in the *New York Herald-Tribune* (R257) called it the best play of the season, but found it "far from completely satisfactory," with "scenes and characters that are more annoying than skillful." Both John Anderson in the *New York Journal-American* (R248) and John Mason Brown in the *Evening Post* (R249) praised Lawrence's performance and remarked that the audience loved both her and the play, but found the play itself not entirely successful.

Burns Mantle in the *New York Daily News* (R254) found *Susan and God* a worthwhile addition to the season, praising the comedy and the good sense illustrated in the play. Like the rest of the critics, he was full of praise for Gertrude Lawrence's radiant performance. Susan Isaacs in *Theatre Arts Monthly* (R251) praised the play as an observant comedy of manners, an idea echoed by Joseph Wood Krutch in *The Nation* (R252). Krutch, however, also found the play ultimately unsatisfying in its intellectual content. The reviewer for *The Commonweal* (R256) had nothing but praise for the play, expressing special enthusiasm for Crothers's moral values and calling *Susan and God* "the most delightful play" of the season.

The filmed version was treated less than kindly by the press. It featured an all-star cast, with Joan Crawford as Susan, Fredric March as Barrie, and Rita Hayworth, Ruth Hussey, Nigel Bruce, John Carroll, Bruce Cabot, Gloria DeHaven and Marjorie Main among the supporting cast. It was directed by George Cukor, with Anita Loos adapting the screenplay from Crothers's play. Metro-Goldwyn-Mayer produced it. Critics found it unsatisfying, however, unable to make its audience care about characters who were found to be unattractive and unappealing.

"Splendor" (Film, 1935)

"Splendor," Crothers's only entirely successful film venture, was made for Samuel Goldwyn Productions in 1935. It was based on an unproduced play, "The House of Lorrimore," which had been deemed too grim and dark-visioned to succeed on Broadway. While the film was directed by Elliott Nugent, Crothers exercised creative control throughout the production, having been involved in both the casting and the choice of director. Thus she managed to avoid the creative frustrations which had marred her other Hollywood ventures.

The Characters--BRIGHTON LORRIMORE: the oldest son of a once-wealthy family now scraping by in the Depression, a man of the highest principles; PHYLLIS LORRIMORE: his bride, a woman from a humble background; MRS. LORRIMORE: the matriarch of the family; CLANCY LORRIMORE: the frivolous younger son; MARTIN DEERING: Brighton's cousin, still financially sucessful despite hard times; EDITH GILBERT: a wealthy young woman in love with Brighton; CLARISSA, CAPTAIN BALLINGER and BILLY GRIMES: the Lorrimores' wealthy friends.

Plot Summary--In an opening scene appropriate for a film made in the midst of the Great Depression the Lorrimore family is seen against a background of luxurious furnishings and stacks of unpaid bills. Only Brighton is upset, however; his mother says it is against her principles to open bills she knows she can't pay, and Clancy, the ne'er-do-well younger brother, only complains about his unreasonable tailor who refuses to produce his new trousers until the old ones are paid for. The only hope of redeeming the fallen Lorrimore fortunes is marriage between Brighton and Edith, a lovely and extremely wealthy young woman who is obviously very much in love with him and eager to redo the family mansion and re-establish their lavish way of life.

Fate and romance have decreed otherwise, however. Brighton clearly has a secret, which, when finally revealed, proves to be his secret marriage to Phyllis, whose considerable naive charm is equalled only by her poverty. Although Phyllis, upon her introduction to the family, is intimidated by their sophistication and lavish surroundings, she is determined to succeed; having always been poor she doesn't mind hard work, she announces to her new mother-in-law, who is not especially impressed by the news. When she informs Brighton that, an experienced seamstress, she means to use her skills to earn a living, he is horrified, insisting that he can and will take care of his entire family by himself. There is no suggestion of how he might do this, however.

Against the background of wealth and privilege provided by the Lorrimores' idle, wealthy friends, Phyllis often looks awkward, but always charming in her obvious sincerity. When Martin Deering, a Lorrimore cousin, shows a marked interest in her she flirts innocently, pleased by his attentiveness, but when he pursues her too aggressively she retreats with the firm statement that she loves her husband, no one else. Martin offers Brighton a job, which he accepts eagerly, but there are strong suggestions that Martin might not be entirely altruistic in his interest.

At a sophisticated poolside party a few weeks later it is clear that Brighton is doing well financially, but not at all clear that he is succeeding on his own merits. The suspicion that Martin doesn't mind having him away on busines ventures deepens; Phyllis, however, is unaware of the gossip which buzzes around them. There are strong suggestions that the senior Mrs. Lorrimore is as eager as Martin to break up the marriage, since she has never liked or approved of Phyllis. When Brighton lands a big job in Mexico the backbiting becomes more aggressive, with the catty Clarissa making several sarcastic comments about his having well-placed friends.

At a later party scene it becomes clear that the entire family suspects Phyllis of selling herself to Martin to insure Brighton's success, although no one wants to confront him because they are all enjoying spending his money. Finally Phyllis can stand no more of the ugly gossip; she insists that Brighton must take no more from Martin, because Martin is really only interested in her. Brighton angrily accuses her of betraying him; she retorts that she was attentive to Martin only because Brighton, and the rest of the Lorrimores, have convinced her that money is more important than anything else. He assures her that money acquired in that way is intolerable, and she runs out of the room.

Desperate over her rejection, Phyllis accepts Martin's invitation to a cruise on his yacht. She is clearly still in love with Brighton, however, and when Martin asks her to marry him she refuses, leaving both him and the Lorrimore world of wealth.

The scene is a chic dress shop, a few months later. A weary-looking Phyllis is seen among the seamstresses. When Edith accidentally discovers her there they talk frankly to each other; Edith suggests that Brighton has not found happiness in the months since Phyllis left. The camera cuts to the Lorrimore home, where Brighton informs his astounded family that he has sold the mansion, the one thing his mother has absolutely refused to contemplate. When she wonders, nearly hysterically, how they are to live, her daughter, Martha, says drily that they will simply have to give up most of the luxuries they had previously enjoyed, just as nearly everyone else has done in this Depression era. The values of independence, self-sufficiency and frugality are discussed, and Brighton begins to realize that he has been to blame for his marital problems, not Phyllis. When Clancy makes an insulting remark Brighton knocks him down and bolts out the door.

In the pelting rain Brighton waits outside the dress shop until Phyllis leaves. He tells her that he has found a newspaper job, and thus a way to use his real talent--writing--instead of pursuing a business career for which he is ill-suited. They profess their love for each other, and forgiveness of the wrongs on both sides, and agree that they will share one--or perhaps two--rooms in happy poverty. "That would be such splendor," Phyllis sighs, and the scene fades to black.

CAST:
> Phyllis Lorrimore--Miriam Hopkins
> Brighton Lorrimore--Joel McCrea
> Martin Deering--Paul Cavanaugh

Mrs. Lorrimore--Helen Westley
Clarissa--Billie Burke
Edith Gilbert--Ruth Weston
Clancy Lorrimore--David Niven (in his first American film role)
Captain Ballinger--Arthur Treacher
Hoffstatter--Torben Meyer
Billy Grimes--Reginald Sheffield

Critical Overview--Reviewers were not kind to the film, finding its material dated and its approach generally ineffective. More than one review declared that the movie dealt with ideas which had already been presented more dramatically in other, recent films.

Primary Bibliography

The first part of this section includes single-text publications of Crothers's plays as well as magazine publications of her one-act plays and anthologies in which her plays were reprinted. The second part indicates libraries in which manuscript copies of her plays are available. The third part is a list of magazine and newspaper articles written by Crothers, designated by the prefix "A." All newspapers are from New York unless otherwise specified. The final part of this section is a list of the principal collections of documents on Crothers.

Full-Length Dramatic Publications

As Husbands Go. New York: Samuel French, 1931.

As Husbands Go. New York: Samuel French 1937.

As Husbands Go. In *Twentieth Century Plays*. Ed. Frank Wadleigh Chandler and Richard Albert Cordell. New York: Thomas Nelson & Sons, 1934.

Caught Wet. New York: Samuel French, 1932.

Everyday. New York: Co-national Plays, Inc., 1930.

Everyday. Minneapolis: Northwestern Press, 1935.

Expressing Willie. Boston: W.H. Baker Co., 1925.

Expressing Willie, Nice People, 39 East. New York: Brentano's, 1924.

Expressing Willie. In *Representative Modern Plays, British and American, From Robertson to O'Neill*. Ed. Richard Cordell. New York: Thomas Nelson & Sons, 1929.

He and She. Boston: W.H. Baker Co., 1933.

He and She. In *Representative American Plays*. Ed. Arthur Hobson Quinn. 5th ed. New York: D. Appleton-Century Co., Inc., 1930.

The Heart of Paddy Whack. New York: Samuel French, 1925.

Let Us Be Gay. New York: Samuel French, 1929.

A Little Journey. New York: Samuel French, 1923.

A Man's World. Boston: R.G. Badger, 1915.

Mary the Third, "Old Lady 31," A Little Journey. New York: Brentano's, 1923.

Mary the Third. Boston: W.H. Baker Co., 1925.

Mary the Third. In *Contemporary Plays*. Ed. Thoms H. Dickinson and Jack R. Crawford. Boston: Houghton Mifflin Co., 1925.

Mary the Third. In *Modern American and British Plays*. Ed. Samuel M. Tucker. New York: Harper and Brothers, 1931.

Mary the Third. In *Modern Plays*. Ed. Samuel Tucker. New York: The Macmillan Co., 1932.

Mary the Third. In *Twenty-five Modern Plays*. Ed. Samuel Tucker. New York: Harper and Brothers, 1931.

Mother Carey's Chickens. New York: Samuel French, 1925. (In collaboration with Kate Douglas Wiggin.)

Nice People. In *Expressing Willie, Nice People, 39 East*. New York: Brentano's, 1924.

Nice People. In *Representative Americn Dramas, National and Local*. Ed. Moses Montrose. Boston: Little, Brown and Co., 1925. Rev. 1933.

"Old Lady 31." In *Mary the Third, "Old Lady 31," A Little Journey*. New York: Brentano's, 1923.

Once Upon a Time. New York: Samuel French, 1925.

Once Upon a Time. In *Contemporary American Plays*. Ed. Arthur Hobson Quinn. New York: Charles Scribner's Sons, 1923.

Susan and God. New York: Dramatists, 1938.

Susan and God. New York: Random House, 1938.

39 East. Boston: W.H. Baker Co., 1925.

39 East. In *Expressing Willie, Nice People, 39 East.* New York: Brentano's, 1924.

The Three of Us. New York: Samuel French, 1916.

When Ladies Meet. New York: Samuel French, 1932.

When Ladies Meet. Acting edition. New York: Samuel French, 1935.

One-Act Plays

PUBLISHED INDIVIDUALLY:

Criss-Cross. New York: Dick and Fitzgerald, 1904.

Peggy. Boston: W.H. Baker Co., 1937.

Peggy. In *Types of Modern Dramatic Composition.* Ed. LeRoy Phillips and Theodore Johnson. Boston: Ginn & Co., 1925.

The Rector. New York: Samuel French, 1905.

The Rector. In *One-Act Plays for Stage and Study.* New York: Samuel French, 1924.

Six One-Act Plays. Boston: W.H. Baker Co., 1925. This volume includes "The Importance of Being a Woman," "The Importance of Being Clothed," "The Importance of Being Married," "The Importance of Being Nice," "Peggy" and "What They Think."

ORIGINAL PUBLICATION OF ONE-ACT PLAYS IN PERIODICALS:

"The Importance of Being Clothed." *Harper's Bazar* June 1920:61+.

"Katy Did." *The Smart Set* Jan. 1909:129-36.

"Mrs. Molly." *The Smart Set* March 1909:104-13.

"Peggy." *Scribner's Magazine* Aug. 1924:175-83.

"What They Think." *The Ladies Home Journal* Feb. 1923:12+.

Manuscripts

A Man's World. Typescript and prompt-book. The Theater Collection, New York Public Library. Typescript Illinois State University, Normal, Ill.

The Coming of Mrs. Patrick. Typescript. Special Collections, Illinois State University Library, Normal, Ill.

He and She. Typescript. The Theater Collection, New York Public Libarary.

The Herfords. Typescript. The Theater Collection, New York Public Library.

"Let Us Be Good." Typescript. The Theater Collection, New York Public Library.

Myself-Bettina. Typescript and prompt-book. Burnside-Frohman Collection, The Theater Collection, New York Public Library.

Nora. Manuscript. Burnside-Frohman Collection, The Theater Collection, New York Public Library.

"Nice People." Film adaptation by Clara Baranger. Shooting script 1922. The Theater Collection, New York Public Library.

"Old Lady 31." Typescript and prompt-book. The Theater Collection, New York Public Library.

Once Upon a Time. The Theater Collection, New York Public Library.

Susan and God. Typescripts of the play and of the 1951 television production. The Theater Collection, New York Public Library.

The Three of Us. Typescript. The Theater Collection, New York Public Library.

When Ladies Meet. Typescript. The Theater Collection, New York Public Library.

Newspaper and Magazine Articles

A01 "The Arts of the Theatre." *Times* 2 Feb. 1919:IV, 2.
    Linked to the production of *A Little Journey*, this article contends that the theater should be the greatest of all the arts, with all of humanity as its model. Crothers also praises modern plays for their natural colloquialism and "quiet realism," better than the artificiality of the past.

A02 "The Construction of a Play." In *The Art of Playwriting*, lectures by Jesse Lynch Williams, Langdon Mitchell, Lord Dunsany, Gilbert Emery and Rachel Crothers. Philadelphia: University of Pennsylvania Press, 1928, pp. 115-34.

Affirms the modern need for plays and films which provide an escape into a world of imagination from a civilization which increasingly "makes life more hideous." Discusses the technical aspects of playwriting.

A03 "Future of the American Stage Depends on Directors." *The New York Times Magazine* 3 Dec. 1916:13.

Says the principal influence on the stage lies with the director, who controls the material, not the author. States that the stage is "inevitably" progressive, given the influence of both radical and conservative forces.

A04 "Here is the 'How,' 'Why' and 'When' of 'Mary the 3rd.'" *Tribune* 25 Feb. 1923.

A discussion of the ideas in a play which dramatizes gaps of understanding between parents and children and the evolution of women's ideas of morally acceptable behavior.

A05 "Notes on the Usages of Charity." *Herald Tribune* 30 Nov. 1932.

An explanation of the goals of the Stage Relief Fund, organized to help theater people hard-hit by the Depression, listing its accomplishments and future plans.

A06 "The Producing Playwright." *Theatre Magazine* Jan. 1918:34.

As many of her essays do, this article emphasizes the necessity for the author to control the direction and production of plays as much as possible, praising many of her co-workers for the freedom she experienced in getting her plays staged. She insists that "work has no sex," that women are as capable as men in directing and producing, if given the chance.

A07 "The Theatre Takes Stock." *Theatre Arts Monthly* May 1940:329.

A brief comment by Crothers, included with six other representatives of the theater, on its present economic condition. Crothers makes a plea for cooperation from all elements in the theatre, labor, producers and artists.

A08 "To the American Theatre." In *Mary the Third, "Old Lady 31," A Little Journey*. New York: Brentano's, 1923.

Praises American "individuality and variety" in stage writing as she expresses a need for more playwriting that is intrinsically American in thought and workmanship. Emphasizes that American drama is less marked by formula and pattern than other traditions.

A09 "Troubles of a Playwright." *Harper's Bazar* Jan. 1911:14-15.
   Emphasizes the importance of casting in the realization of a playwright's vision, stressing the difficulties of the process and praising many of the actors and producers she has worked with.

A10 "The War and the Women of Our Stage." *Times* 27 May 1917.
   Describes the foundation of the Stage Women's War Relief Project, originated by Crothers and several other women prominent in the theater in an effort to alleviate some of the war-related suffering in Europe.

A11 "Whence Came Susan?" *Times* 7 Nov. 1937:X, 3.
   Crothers states that the idea for *Susan and God* came to her while she pondered questions of belief and meaning in these dark days. She compares Susan, "vain, silly, foolish and spoiled," to the modern world, shattered by failure and desperately needing something to believe in. She contends that the world, like Susan, could see goodness dominate "if only we'd let it."

A12 "Woman and the Theatre." *Boston Evening Transcript* 14 Feb. 1912.
   A transcript of an address by Crothers before the Boston Drama League, on the occasion of *The Herfords'* being performed in that city. Crothers speaks out strongly on the idea of women as both the subject of and the audience for plays, especially praising women's taste for experimentation and for serious subjects in drama. She defends "bold or daring" plays even if they are to be seen by young people, insisting that young men and women "might be saddened or enlightened but never hurt" by honest, forthright theater.

Collections of Documents

Coverage of Crothers by the press, including reviews, articles, speeches and other documents pertaining to her career, can be found in several sources. The most significant are:

1. Substantial and varied holdings in the Theater Collection of the New York Public Library. This includes the Robinson Locke Collection, an invaluable compilation of scrapbooks filed under the names of actors and actresses who appeared in the plays, as well as the author's name. Other collections of clippings are also found in the Theater Collection under the names of actors and actresses as well as the titles of individual plays. Several typescripts of her plays, as mentioned above, are also in the Theater Collection.

2. Three volumes of scrapbooks compiled in 1953 by Irving Abrahamson from material collected by Crothers's family, mainly reviews of the plays and articles by and about the author. The volumes are available on microfilm from the University of Chicago Library.

3. The Crothers Collection at Milner Library, Illinois State University, Normal, Ill. This contains, along with the typescripts mentioned above, the scrapbooks assembled by Abrahamson and another scrapbook assembled by Crothers herself, as well as a folder of clippings and correspondence pertaining to the production of some of her plays.

4. The Crothers Collection at the Bloomington Public Library, Bloomington, Ill. This is a collection of clippings from the *Daily Pantagraph* pertaining to Crothers's family and career.

Annotated Secondary Bibliography

The following is an annotated bibliography of reviews of Crothers's Broadway productions and significant productions on tour, as well as substantial interviews and articles spanning her career, and listings in reference works. The bibliography is chronologically ordered. Most of the selections are reviews or feature articles on individual productions and are identified by the prefix "R"; interviews are indicated by the prefix "I" and articles in reference works and other full-length studies are indicated by the prefix "B."

Since most of the material on Crothers is available only from newspaper clippings, on microfilm or in scrapbooks, page numbers are often impossible to obtain; they are included when possible. Many other reviews of Crothers's work exist; since they are often unidentified clippings or scrapbook entries they are not included in the bibliography. They can be found when pursuing studies of the individual plays, actors or actresses. All newspapers listed are from New York unless otherwise indicated.

1906-1915

1906

R001 "Another Western Drama to the Fore." *World* 18 Oct. 1906.
> The reviewer predicts that Broadway newcomer Crothers is "destined to win prolonged success," declaring that she has broken the jinx of unsuccessful offerings that had plagued the Madison Square Theatre.

R002 Corbin, John. "Realism in 'The Three of Us.'" *Sun* 18 Oct. 1906.
> Gives the play high praise for its "fidelity to the unaffected truth of daily life" and avoidance of sensationalism. There are no red flannel shirts or whiskey-drinking cowboys, but "one felt the very pinch of poverty and the corrosion of hope deferred."

R003   Dale, Alan. "Alan Dale Says: 'Don't Let The Two of You Miss "The Three of Us."'" *American* 18 Oct. 1906.
   Dale says the play is flawless, praising the moral, the acting, the casting and the author's vision. It is "exquisitely modulated," "subtly and fragrantly vitriolic," "deliciously natural" and "poignantly dramatic."

R004   Hennessey, Roland Burke. "Carlotta Nillson Shows Fine Emotionalism In That Very Human Play 'The Three of Us." *News* 18 Oct. 1906.
   Praises the "rugged strength," the sense of the wide-openness of Western life, the idealism and the effective portrait of a fighting woman in the play.

R005   Leslie, Amy. "Garrick Has A Winner." *Chicago News* 3 June 1906.
   Praises the play for its poetic style and ethical nobility as well as its effective structure.

R006   McCay, Frederic Edward. "Carlotta Nillson Scores in a Realistic Drama." *Mail* 18 Oct. 1906.
   Proclaims Carlotta Nillson the new star, Rachel Crothers the new dramatist, and William Lawrence the new manager of the future for presenting this wonderful hit.

R007   "Miss Nillson Triumphs in 'The Three of Us.'" *Press* 18 Oct. 1906.
   Enthusiastic praise for the acting, the vision, the wholesomeness of the play, which "leaped into success" in the first act and stayed there.

R008   "The New Plays." *Toledo Blade* 24 Jan. 1906.
   Strong praise for a new play and a new playwright.

I009   Quimby, Harriet. "Triumph of a Struggling Actress--Carlotta Nillson's Success." *Leslie's Weekly* 8 Nov. 1906:446.
   In a lengthy interview with the star of *The Three of Us* Quimby praises both Nillson and Crothers for this refreshing new entry on the American stage.

R010   "The Theater." *Louisville Herald* 8 March 1906.
   Praises the play extravagantly, especially citing its true feeling, the originality of its concept and its genuine power.

R011   "The Three of Us." *Blue Book* Dec. 1906.
   Especially praises the fresh Americanness of the play, which is realistic without being sordid or depressing.

R012   "The Three of Us." *Kansas City Post* 25 Feb. 1906.
   Commends Crothers for dealing honestly and straightforwardly with what might have been only conventionally melodramatic material.

R013 "The Three of Us." *St. Louis Star* 11 Feb. 1906.
   Finds little to praise in the play, finding it overlong and tiresome.

R014 "The Three of Us." *Theatre Magazine* Dec. 1906:316-17.
   Despite judging that this is not a "well-built" or especially original play the reviewer praises its simplicity and genuine emotion, concluding that *The Three of Us* promises great things for the future of its young author, who has "the eyes of love for human nature."

R015 "'Three of Us' is a 'Lucky Strike.'" *Herald* 18 Oct. 1906.
   The freshness and originality of Crothers's realism and the strength of the acting are praised.

R016 "Two Playwrights and Their Methods." *Times* 22 Oct. 1906.
   A profile article compares Crothers, the newcomer, with William Gillette, an established success, in Crothers's favor. The naturalness and realism, the absence of "commonplace trickery of the stage," the appeal to the heart and the forthright honesty of both the play and the acting are especially singled out for praise.

1907

R017 "The Coming of Mrs. Patrick." *Evening Post* 17 Nov. 1907.
   Praises the picture of the generous Mrs. Patrick but finds the play crude and poorly structured.

R018 "The Coming of Mrs. Patrick." *Times* 7 Nov. 1907, sec. 5:1. In *The New York Times Theater Reviews 1904-1911*.
   The reviewer declares that Crothers's reputation, so well established with her first Broadway venture, is not enhanced by this play, finding the furniture the most interesting component.

R019 "Madison Square: The Coming of Mrs. Patrick." *Theatre Magazine* Dec. 1907.
   Praises the play's attempts at originality, finding its merits more noteworthy than its flaws.

R020 "Reviews of New Plays." *Mirror* 16 Nov. 1907.
   Finds the play reasonably interesting but too slow, with more dialogue than action.

R021 "The Thaumaturgic Mrs. Patrick." *Telegram* 7 Nov. 1907.
   Finds the play "feeble" and "feminine," fairly interesting but too slow-moving. Comments on an audience either bored or laughing at inappropriate moments.

1908

R022   Darnton, Charles. "Maxine Elliott Fails as a Tiresome New England Magda." *Evening World* 6 Oct. 1908.
    Darnton is especially negative on the subject of the play's sexuality, which he finds excessive and gratuitous.

R023   "Maxine Elliott as a Selfish Sister." *Times* 6 Oct. 1908, sec. 9:3. In *The New York Times Theater Reviews 1904-1911*.
    Finds the play interesting but poorly timed; Crothers's ideas have been done recently, and better, by other dramatists.

R024   "Maxine Elliott in 'Myself--Bettina.'" *Tribune* 6 Oct. 1908.
    Finds the play vulgar and anti-feminine, one of the season's worst offerings.

R025   "Miss Elliott in a New Comedy." *Philadelphia Inquirer* 22 Sept. 1908.
    Praises the star's audience appeal but finds the play didactic and sentimental, while conceding that the audience seems to like it.

R026   "Myself-Bettina." *Blue Book* Nov. 1908.
    Finds the play a failure, wondering rhetorically what the author is doing with her talent.

R027   "Myself--Bettina." *Theatre Magazine* Nov. 1908:xii.
    Finds the play insignificant, inconclusive and unconvincing.

R028   "Myself--Bettina." *Toledo Blade* 10 March 1908.
    Finds the play didactic and embarrassing, although praising the star and finding praise for Crothers's other work.

R029   "A New England 'Magda.'" *Sun* 6 Oct. 1908.
    Calls the play a disappointment, derivative and insincere.

R030   Pierce, Lucy France. "Women Who Write Plays." *World Today* July 1908:725-31.
    Considers women playwrights as gaining new power and recognition in a field previously dominated by men. Praises Crothers for her logic, her craftsmanship, her sincerity and conviction.

1909-1911

R031   "'As a Man Thinks'--The Masterpiece of America's Leading Playwright." *Current Literature* May 1911.
    Considering Augustus Thomas's play the review concedes the playwright's stature but finds the play too didactic, and questions the

New York critics' overwhelming praise for Thomas.

R032 "Augustus Thomas Excels His Previous Efforts." *New York Review* May
1911.
Calls *As a Man Thinks* "exceptionally gratifying, about as fine an
achievement" in playwriting as the "English-speaking theater has
produced."

R033 "The Drama." *The Nation* 10 Feb. 1910:146.
Calls *A Man's World* "one of the strongest, most interesting, logical
and dramatic pieces on the now dominant topic of the relations of the
sexes." The reviewer especially praises Crothers for her fairness and
courage in refusing to sacrifice truth to "sentiment, or the desire for a
happy ending."

R034 "Free Tickets for Mary Mannering's Latest Play." *Detroit News-Tribune*
7 Nov. 1909.
Praising the play's timeliness, the paper offers 18 pairs of free tickets
to women theatergoers.

R035 "Garrick." *Detroit Times* 9 Nov. 1909.
Listing *A Man's World* under the name of the theatre, the review
praises Crothers for the strength of her characters.

R036 Gibson, Idah McGlone. "Mac's Gossip of the Stage." *Toledo Blade* 14
May 1910.
Praises the play extravagantly, especially for its unsparing realism in
presenting the relationship between the sexes. Calls Crothers the
country's best dramatist.

R037 "A Man's World." *Chicago Record* 11 May 1910.
Finds the play weak, improbable and unoriginal.

R038 "A Man's World." *Everybody's Magazine* January 1910.
Praises the controversial subject of the play but finds the characters
somewhat confusingly conceived by the author.

R039 "'A Man's World': Fine Theme Well Handled." *Times* 9 Feb. 1910,
sec.5:2. In *The New York Times Theater Reviews 1904-1911.*
Praises the play for being both moral and entertaining, but says even
its eloquence won't change the fact that this is indeed a man's world.

R040 "'A Man's World' Produced at the Comedy Theatre." *Daily Tribune* 9
Feb. 1910.
Objects to the message of the play, finding it obvious and one-sided.
Mary Mannering's acting is called ordinary and without conviction;
even the audience is criticized for being too ready with its applause on

points that, according to the reviewer, it did not understand properly.

R041 "'A Man's World' Shows Big Problem." *Philadelphia Times* 12 April 1910.
    Praises the play's idea but finds it ultimately unconvincing, stating that women are apt to let their hearts rule their heads rather than the other way around.

R042 Mary Mannering in 'A Man's World.'" *Cincinnati Inquirer* 14 Nov. 1909.
    Finds the play gripping and entertaining, if not entirely convincing in its presentation of the relationship of the sexes.

R043 "Ministers are Enthusiastic for 'A Man's World.'" *New York City Review* 5 March 1910.
    Discusses the "exceptional indorsements" the play has received from "the leading clergymen of New York City" and from other cities where it had toured. Several letters are quoted in full.

R044 "Ministers at Theater." *Philadelphia Record* 10 April 1910.
    Praises the play for its moral stature, mentioning that local clergy had been invited to attend *A Man's World* free of charge.

R045 "Miss Mannering in Absorbing Play." *Buffalo Evening News* 22 Oct. 1909.
    Praises the play's realism and the acting, especially of Mannering.

R046 "Miss Mannering in Forceful New Play." *Buffalo Evening Times* 22 Oct. 1909.
    Praises the power and originality of *A Man's World*, along with the strength of the acting.

R047 "Miss Mannering in Her New Role." *St. Louis* (Mo.) *Republic* 30 Nov. 1909.
    Praises *A Man's World* but is more interested in the fashionable members of the audience, "one of the most socially distinguished of the season," whose names are listed at the end of the review.

I048 Patterson, Ada. "Woman Must Live Out Her Destiny." *The Theatre Magazine* May 1910:134, 136.
    An interview in which an outspoken Crothers emphasizes that a playwright must have "the courage of the unhappy ending" in order to have a character "live out her destiny." Crothers defines herself as a realist who knows plays will not reform the world, but who means to provide serious, thought-provoking material.

R049 "Plays of the Month: 'A Man's World.'" *Theatre Arts Magazine* March 1910:68-69.

In a review which is largely a summary of the plot, Mary Mannering is praised for having "outgrown mere prettiness" and taken on a challenging role. She "has never played any other part with just this same kind of feeling." The "man of the double standard," however, is found "a touch too brutal in feeling."

R050 Winter, William. "A Great Play Greatly Acted." *Harper's Weekly* May 1911.

In an extensive review article on Augustus Thomas's "As a Man Thinks" Winter praises both play and playwright extravagantly, praising its profound philosophy and its absolute rightness on the subject of the relation between the sexes.

1912

I051 Patterson, Ada. "Miss Rachel Crothers." *Journal* 25 May 1912.

In an interview Crothers predicts that women's force will soon be felt in government, contending that they should especially influence education.

R052 "Players and the Plays: 'The Herfords.'" *Christian Science Monitor* 25 Jan. 1912.

This long, thoughtful review article praises Crothers for the "delicacy of touch" and depth of feeling with which she addresses the "unsolvable riddle" of whether a woman should be "a homemaker for some man" or a person in her own right. It praises Crothers for deciding in favor of the "truism that a true mother will choose the welfare of her child above everything else."

1913

I053 "Girls Need 'Big Sisters.'" *Tribune* 17 Nov. 1913.

In a lengthy interview Crothers expresses herself forcefully on the subject of rescuing troubled girls before they are placed in institutions like reformatories. She underlines the need for individual effort, not impersonal institutions.

R054 "The New Plays: 'Ourselves.'" *The Theatre Magazine* Dec. 1913:xviii.

Calls the play notable, among plays of the feminist movement, not so much for its conclusiveness as for its excellence in skill as a play. "It is not meant to please, not meant as idle enjoyment," but it still holds the attention every minute of its duration.

R055 "'Ourselves' is a Gripping Play." *Times* 14 Nov. 1913.

Calls the play powerful but not timely, a "gripping, living drama" which deals with a subject theatergoers may have grown tired of. Crothers is praised for her tact in dealing with a taboo subject without "an objectionable line or a repulsive situation" in any moment of the play.

R056 "'Ourselves' Strong Argument for Reforming Girls." *Evening Journal* 14 Nov. 1913.
Praises the play for its courageous, convincing presentation of a crucial modern problem.

R057 "The Real Sex Problem." *Tribune* 14 Nov.1913.
Focuses especially on the audience, which "sat spellbound for four grueling acts," except when it "burst into tumultuous applause." Finds the play strong and convincing.

1914

R058 "Charming Comedy is 'Young Wisdom.'" *Times* 6 Jan. 1914.
Praises the lighthearted comedy and the acting, especially the Taliaferro sisters in the lead roles. Mentions the enthusiasm of the audience, especially in summoning the author at the curtain call.

R059 "The Gossoon and the Goose." *Washington Star* 10 Oct. 1914.
Praises the acting of both Chauncey Olcott and Edith Luckett in *The Heart of Paddy Whack*, finding the play a delight.

R060 "The Heart of Paddy Whack." *Rochester* (New York) *Post Express* 18 Nov. 1914.
Praises both the production and its star lavishly, calling the play one of Chauncey Olcott's best.

R061 "The Heart of Paddy Whack." *Times* 24 Nov. 1914, col. 13:5. In *The New York Times Theater Reviews 1912-1919.*
Praises star Chauncey Olcott for challenging himself dramatically, calling this play "the best in which he has been seen."

R062 "Miss Crothers' Play Delights." *New York City Press* 6 Jan. 1914.
Calls *Young Wisdom* the "greatest joke of the theatrical season" on the audience, which has come to expect serious, ethical discussion from Crothers, and instead was delighted by this "hugely funny, wholesome preachment" on the subject of youth, which is forever being treated too seriously.

R063 "Miss Crothers Play Hit in Chicago." (Bloomington, Ill.) *Pantagraph* 23 Feb. 1914.
Crothers's hometown paper finds high praise for *Young Wisdom,*

calling it delightful entertainment with "light satire and a pretty sentiment."

R064 "New Comedy Well Suited to Taliaferro Sisters." *Herald* 6 Jan. 1914.
Focuses on the high quality of the acting, especially the Taliaferro sisters, who are said to have reached star status with *Young Wisdom*.

R065 "The New Plays." *Telegram* 24 Nov. 1914.
Finds the story very slight, but praises Chauncey Olcott for his irresistible charm in *The Heart of Paddy Whack*.

R066 "Olcott Romantic in 'Paddy Whack.'" *Hartford* (Conn.) *Courant* 21 Dec. 1914.
Calls the play bright and entertaining, with quaint and charming dialogue, but finds it predictable and overlong.

R067 "Olcott's New Piece." *Variety* 7 Oct. 1914.
Praises *The Heart of Paddy Whack* for affording Chauncey Olcott the chance to age gracefully and effectively.

R068 "The Plays." *Brooklyn Eagle* 24 Nov. 1914.
Praises Chauncey Olcott extravagantly for his performance in *The Heart of Paddy Whack*, emphasizing the durability of his charm for the audience.

R069 St. John-Brenon, Algernon. "Taliaferros Do Well as Stars." *Telegram* 6 Jan 1914.
Calls *Young Wisdom* a delightful, exhilarating comedy, a successful burlesque of the "cant and sentimentality current among young women doctors of philosophy who possess that little and narrowly focussed knowledge of life which is so dangerous."

R070 "Taliaferros Co-Star; Sisters Make a Broadway Hit in Bright Comedy." *Sun* 6 Jan. 1914.
Says the plot of *Young Wisdom* is ordinary but the play redeemed by its bright comedy and by providing a star vehicle for such fine performers as the Taliaferro sisters.

R071 "Taliaferros in 'Young Wisdom.'" *Morning Telegraph* 6 Jan.1914.
Praises the play's broadly humorous, delightful satire of contemporary mores.

R072 "Taliaferros in 'Young Wisdom.'" *Philadelphia Public Ledger* 31 March 1914.
Dislikes the play's attack on "old-fashioned matrimony," criticizing it for failing to suggest solutions for the problems it makes fun of.

R073 "Young Wisdom." *Boston Transcript* 8 Jan.1914.
      Praises the comedy and bright satire of the play, mentioning the enthusiastic audience.

R074 "Young Wisdom." *Theatre Magazine* Feb. 1914:32.
      Finds the play one of the season's best; praises Crothers for taking the ideas of a "problem play" and turning them into a delightful comedy with a light, refined touch, "imbued with feminine delicacy."

R075 "'Young Wisdom,' at the Criterion, is a Great Big Triple Success." *Evening Journal* 7 Jan. 1914.
      Praises Crothers as a "militant champion of all that modern feminism demands," and also for being able to take those demands lightly, achieving comic success.

R076 "'Young Wisdom' Is a Brilliant Comedy." *Brooklyn Eagle* 6 Jan. 1914.
      Calls this a popular hit which equals *The Three of Us* in its ability to make a serious point with humor.

R077 "'Young Wisdom' is Bright and Pleasing." *Mail* 6 Jan. 1914.
      Finds the play mild but pleasing, with good satire and fine acting.

R078 "Young Wisdom So Good Critics Find a Sinecure: It's Just One Bright Spot." *Atlanta Journal* 4 Nov.1914.
      Praises the play's uproarious comedy and its clever satire of modern ideas.

1915

I079 Marshall, Marguerite Mooers. "What Do Women Think of Other Women." *Minneapolis Journal* 29 March 1915.
      In an interview Crothers is quoted as saying that women still have a long way to go to achieve social equality. She urges women to think of issues besides clothes and personal matters, challenging them to work creatively, to form strong friendships with other women, to "learn to be as generous with one another as men are."

1916-1920

1916

R080 "After the Play." *The New Republic* 23 Dec. 1916, 9:217-18.
      Calls *"Old Lady 31"* courageous, but says it makes concessions; because it deals with age, an unpopular subject, Crothers has "sugared it up" for her Broadway audience. There is sweetness, pathos and wisdom in the play, but the "stupid conventionality" of the ending weakens its effect.

R081 Broun, Heywood. "In Wigs and Wings." *Tribune* 5 Nov. 1916.
    In a second look at *"Old Lady 31"* for the Sunday edition, Broun examines in detail the combination of delightful humor, pleasing sentiment and easy teaching of "a great moral lesson in the play," calling it "the important event of the season."

R082 Broun, Heywood. "'Old Lady 31' Sheer Delight." *Tribune* 31 Oct. 1916.
    Praises the "rare discretion" with which Crothers handle the combination of "sunshine and sentiment" in the play, calling it a rare comedy of character.

R083 Darnton, Charles. "The New Plays." *Evening World* 2 Nov. 1916.
    Praises *"Old Lady 31"* as a "simple, tear-stirring little comedy" which will appeal to the heart as well as to the sense of humor.

R084 DeFoe, Louis V. "A Sunshine Comedy of the Twilight of Life." *World* 31 Oct. 1916.
    Praises the play as the best thing since *Mrs. Wiggs of the Cabbage Patch*; like most reviewers, DeFoe is especially impressed by the skill with which Crothers mixes humor and sentiment. He also praises her skill and originality in casting.

I085 "Future of American Stage Depends on Directors." *New York Times Magazine* 3 Dec. 1916:13.
    An extended interview with Crothers, who was directing *"Old Lady 31,"* emphasizes the variety of her talents and praises her strong-minded control of her material. Crothers's views on the future of the theater in Europe and America are quoted extensively.

R086 "Miss Emma Dunn Wins Stellar Honors in Novel 'Old Lady 31.'" *Herald* 31 Oct. 1916.
    Praises the play for avoiding the easy glamour of youthful subjects and providing truly sound American entertainment in its presentation of old people.

R087 Mullin, Howard B. "Cynics, After Seeing 'Old Lady 31,' Warn Others to Weep." *Herald* 19 Nov. 1916.
    In a two-page illustrated feature article Mullin finds high praise for the moral values presented in the play. He includes excerpts from several scenes and an interview with Emma Dunn, the star.

R088 "'Old Lady 31.'" *Theatre Magazine* Dec. 1916:357.
    Like most reviews this one is filled with enthusiasm for the effective humor and skillfully controlled sentiment of the play. However it finds the roles and the acting of the juvenile leads ineffective, adding a "jarring note" to an otherwise effective production. The review is ecstatic over Dunn, however, praising her voice and her artistry.

R089 "'Old Lady 31' A Play Full of Laughter." *Times* 31 Oct. 1916, col. 11:1. In *The New York Times Theater Reviews 1912-1919*.
  Calls the play a "homely, gentle, pathetic, shrewd little comedy," praising its control of sentiment.

R090 "'Old Lady 31' is a Pronounced Hit." *Journal of Commerce* 2 Nov. 1916.
  Finds the play sincere, filled with pathos and good, honest laughter. A pronounced success.

R091 Sherwin, Louis. "'Old Lady 31' at the Thirty-Ninth Street." *Globe and Commercial Advertiser* 2 Nov. 1916.
  Finds the play the biggest surprise of the season: who would expect a play whose action "takes place mostly in an Old Ladies Home" to be the best entertainment of the season? Sherwin fully expected to hate the play, he asserts; instead he enjoyed its genuine emotion, buoyant humor and skillful dialogue. "Decidedly all hats are off to Miss Crothers," he concludes.

R092 Woollcott, Alexander. "Second Thoughts on First Nights." *Times* 5 Nov. 1916, col. 11:6:1. In *The New York Times Theater Reviews 1912-1919*.
  Giving the play a thoughtful second look Woollcott praises Crothers's skill in adapting the story by Louise Forsslund, adding "her own wit and wisdom" to an excellent source.

1917

R093 "Mother Carey and Her Chickens." *Times* 26 Sept. 1917, col. 11:1. In *The New York Times Theater Reviews 1912-1919*.
  While the review expresses reservations about plays which contrast rural and urban characters and find that all virtue resides in rusticity, it concludes that Crothers and Wiggin meet the challenge in an entertaining, sweet play.

R094 "Mother Carey's Chickens." *Herald* 26 Sept. 1917.
  Praises Crothers's adaptation, comparing it to the play version of *Little Women.*

R095 "Mother Carey's Chickens." *Evening Journal* 26 Sept. 1917.
  Mentioning the delighted audience, the review finds the play charming, filled with delightful characters and pleasing sentiment.

R096 "The New Plays." *Evening Telegram* 26 Sept. 1917.
  Praising Crothers as one of America's leading dramatists, the review especially commends her for providing a change from "lurid melodrama and libidinous musical comedy" in *Mother Carey's Chickens.*

R097 "Providence Opera House." *Providence Journal* 19 Sept. 1917.
Praises the skill with which Crothers transferred the popular novel *Mother Carey's Chickens* to the stage. Mentions the "slender plot" but praises the atmosphere.

R098 "Rachel Crothers's New Play Success." *Brooklyn Eagle* 26 Sept. 1917.
Praises the play for adding a note of brightness in a world which is filled with darkness.

R099 "The Theater Women's War-Work." *The Literary Digest* 16 June 1917.
An overview article on the subject of dramatists and their work for the war effort, mostly quoted from Crothers, who headed the project.

R100 "Theatrical Review." *Hartford* (Conn.) *Post* 24 Jan. 1917.
While finding *Mother Carey's Chickens* a bit sweet and awkwardly structured, the review praises the acting and says the play provides a pleasant evening, with some brilliant lines and a cheerful sentiment

1918

R101 Broun, Heywood. "The New Plays." *Tribune* 27 Dec. 1918.
Finds *A Little Journey* amusing and pleasing, but not entirely satisfying or convincing.

R102 Broun, Heywood. "Olcott Shows to Advantage in Comedy Scenes of His New Play." *Tribune* 17 April 1918.
Broun congratulates Olcott on adding a new dimension to his career, proving his ability in light comedy instead of remaining a popular crowd-pleaser.

R103 Collins, Charles. "Chauncey Olcott in Irish Comedy." *Chicago Evening Post* 5 March 1918.
While finding *Once Upon a Time* a bit too "stage-Irish," the review praises Olcott and mentions his popularity with the audience.

R104 Corbin, John. "Drama: 'A Little Journey.'" *Times* 27 Dec. 1918.
While Corbin is only mildly pleased by the play, which he finds a bit sentimental, he likes the comedy supplied by the type-characters.

R105 Darnton, Charles. "Chauncey Olcott 'Feeds the Child.'" *Evening World* 17 April 1918.
Praises Olcott for taking risks with his career in *Once Upon a Time,* especially for leaving youthful roles behind and succeeding in more mature comedy.

R106   Darnton, Charles. "The New Plays: 'A Little Journey' A Sentimental Tour." *Evening World* 27 Dec. 1918.

Finds rare humor and simple human feeling, as well as impressive emotions of "understanding and belief" developing out of the situation of the train wreck. Cyril Keightley's acting is praised but Estelle Winwood as Julie is "cold and matter-of-fact" in her manner.

R107   "A Little Journey." *Herald* 27 Dec. 1918.

Praises the play for its breadth of emotion and human feeling, calling it "an adventure of the soul" which made the audience reluctant to leave at the end.

R108   "A Little Journey." *Post* 27 Dec. 1918.

Finds the play of mixed quality, with a wandering plot and improbable situations, but mentions how much the audience enjoyed it.

R109   Mantle, Burns. "A Little Journey." *Daily Mail* 27 Dec. 1918.

Praises the play for its acute observation of character and Crothers for her skill in plotting, casting and directing. Estelle Winwood in the lead role receives special mention for her ability to win the audience.

R110   "Once Upon a Time." *Theatre Magazine* May 1918:316.

Considers the play primarily as a vehicle for Olcott, giving him an "opportunity to sing some of the Irish songs that he does so well," but calls the child star, Bonnie Marie, the real hit of the evening.

R111   "Real Pleasure in 'A Little Journey.'" *Evening Sun* 27 Dec. 1918.

Finds the play an amusing light comedy but rather hackneyed, one of a number of plays dealing with regeneration this season. Says it's worth "a little journey" to the delightful Little Theatre, but "hardly worth a long journey there."

1919

R112   Baker, Colgate. "'39 East' & Constance Binney Unadulterated Joy." *Review* 1 April 1919.

Congratulates Messrs. Lee and J.J. Shubert on presenting "one of the happiest events of the season," delighting in the sweet innocence of the heroine, the convincing fairytale quality of the plot, and the acting of the entire cast, especially Constance Binney. The producers are especially commended for supplying such delightful, wholesome entertainment.

R113   Corbin, John. "Drama: Wistaria Romance." *Times* 1 April 1919, col. 9:1. In *The New York Times Theater Reviews 1912-1919*.

Finds *39 East* unpretentious and humorous, filled with good acting which pleased an enthusiastic audience.

R114 Corbin, John. "The Play With a Nudge." *Times* 6 April 1919, IV:2:1.
        In a comprehensive Sunday article Corbin assesses the ways
    playwrights can reach across the footlights to "nudge" the audience,
    manipulating them into accepting the play's ideas. Considers Crothers,
    J.M. Barrie and Clyde Fitch masters of this art, finding special praise for
    Crothers's subtlety. Corbin does, however, suggest that Crothers might
    bring more emotional range to future endeavors; she is "so resolutely the
    miniaturist that she avoids the situation dramatic."

R115 Dale, Allan. "'39 East,' at the Broadhurst, a Comedy. " *American* 1 April
    1919.
        Unconvinced by the sentimental love story of naivete and virtue,
    Dale finds the play "very feeble material," though he concedes that
    Constance Binney is "cute" in the lead role.

R116 Darnton, Charles. "'39 East' A Heart-Warming Comedy." *Evening World*
    1 April 1919.
        Calls the play true in its observation of life and sympathetic in its
    treatment of character types, "the best romantic comedy since 'The
    Cinderella Man.'"

R117 DeFoe, Louis V. "Sentimental Play Tinctured With Fun." *World* 1 April
    1919.
        In a long, enthusiastic review DeFoe defends *39 East* against a
    possible charge of being "irritatingly adorable," finding it instead gently
    and wisely satirical, with an appealing romance and much observation of
    real human nature. He includes Crothers's last two plays, *A Little
    Journey* and *"Old Lady 31,"* in his analysis, finding in them praiseworthy
    use of "the old expedients and devices of the ingenious and expert"
    playwright. He considers Crothers along with Clare Kummer and Rita
    Wellman, two other successful woman playwrights, finding *39 East* the
    "cleverest play by a woman" of the current season.

R118 Finck, Henry T. "39 East." *Post* 1 April 1919.
        Praises the play for its originality of invention and for its "snappy, if
    somewhat conventional," dialogue.

R119 "A Little Journey." *Theatre Magazine* Feb. 1919:77.
        Although the story is tenuous for a full evening's entertainment, and
    there is "palpable effort in the introduction of episodic details," the
    freshness of characterization and the wit and snap of the dialogue are
    praised.

R120 Mantle, Burns. "'39 East' Tells of a Minister's Daughter Who Didn't Go
    Wrong." *Mail* 1 April 1919.
        Praises Crothers's keen observation and warm emotions, finding her
    the perfect playwright to deal with the type characters in a play like this,

although suggesting gently that plays about "innocents abroad in New York" have become fairly commonplace. All of the acting receives praise, especially that of Constance Binney and Henry Hull, the juvenile leads.

R121   Price, Frank J. "'39 East' is a Play of Love." *Evening Telegram* 1 April 1919.
Predicts permanent popularity for the play, based on the enthusiasm of the audience's response to Crothers's curtain call and to the play as a whole.

R122   "Sentiment is the Dominant Note in the Latest Output From Rachel Crothers's Indefatigable Pen." *Theatre Magazine* May 1919.
While finding that *39 East* fails to measure up to the "most exacting standards of modern dramaturgy," the review finds it graceful and entertaining, and notes the acting promise of Constance Binney in the lead role.

R123   "'39 East' and 'Take it From Me' Both Score." *Globe and Commercial Advertiser* 1 April 1919.
While calling it "a naive combination of dime thriller, fairy tale" and sensational novel, the review found the play an enjoyable, comic presentation of recognizable types.

1920

R124   Broun, Heywood. "'He and She' Puts Woman in Her Place." *Tribune* 13 Feb. 1920.
Treats Crothers's ideas with respect but disagrees with them, finding them "antifeminist" and pessimistic. He contends that the ending is too bleak, but praises Crothers's persistence in getting the play on stage and acting its lead role.

R125   Dale, Alan. "He and She." *American* 13 Feb. 1920.
Dale is mostly negative and condescending in this play, finding its thesis the subject for jokes rather than serious consideration. He praises the attempt at addressing a serious issue, but finds the play unconvincing.

R126   Darnton, Charles. "He and She." *Evening World* 13 Feb. 1920.
Praises the play for the restraint and objectivity with which it makes its points, finding it an engrossing evening of theater.

R127   Dickenson, Weed. "'He and She' at Little Theater." *Morning Telegraph* 13 Feb. 1920.
Finds the play comic in its pretensions rather than serious, mocking both the bleakness of Crothers's picture and the audience who accepted

its ideas. Does praise the play's structure and dialogue.

R128 "Feminine Problem in 'He and She.'" *Herald* 13 Feb. 1920.
    Calls the play far-fetched and implies that the problem it deals with
is primarily imaginary, or at best insignificant. Finds Crothers intelligent
but tense and nervous as an actress in the lead role.

R129 "He and She." *The Call* 13 Feb. 1920.
    Praises the comedy of the play but finds it unconvincing and overly
unkind to men, mocking the pessimism of the ending especially.

R130 MacGowan, Kenneth. "Curtain Calls: when Playwrights Dissertate on
    Home and Children." *Globe and Commercial Advertiser* 15 Feb. 1920.
    This review article compares *He and She* with another "problem
play," *The Famous Mrs. Fair*, by James Forbes, finding the former
marginally more entertaining but the latter more emotionally satisfying.
Crothers is criticized for letting her thesis dominate her writing ability,
and for creating a situation "for its polemic value," not because it's
especially probable or even entertaining.

R131 MacGowan, Kenneth. "The New Play." *Globe and Commercial
    Advertiser* 13 Feb. 1920.
    Complaining that thesis plays are dreary and difficult both to see and
to write about, MacGowan finds that Crothers loses control of her
material, letting her ideas dominate to the detriment of her dramatic
sense. The lengthy review is almost entirely negative, finding fault with
Crothers's ability as an actress as well as her "schoolma'amy tendency
to say the obvious thing obviously in the first act and occasionally in the
second."

R132 Mantle, Burns. "The Theater." *Evening Mail* 13 Feb. 1920.
    Mantle praises Crothers's development of ideas in *He and She*,
contending that the controversial ending is justified by the fact that
society itself has not yet found an equitable way for women to combine
family with career.

R133 "Miss Crothers's Latest Play." *Evening Sun* 13 Feb. 1920.
    Finds that "poor old Feminism never had a chance" in *He and She*,
but calls it interesting, with good dialogue and character development.

R134 "Mr. Hornblow Goes to the Play." *Theatre Magazine* April 1920:269-70.
    Says that Crothers is so purposeful, so observant and so true in her
characterization that no play of hers fails to be compelling. *He and She,*
however, is found ultimately unconvincing, too episodic and
exaggerated. Crothers's acting, as well as that of Faire Binney as her
daughter, is praised.

R135 "New Play About Duties of a Wife." *Globe and Commercial Advertiser* 13 Feb. 1920.

Calls the play an exhibition of one woman's versatility because Crothers is both author and actress, but finds its "contention that a husband is his wife's master and overseer now pretty much exploded." Finds the play unconvincing and tedious, if occasionally effective in its writing.

R136 Towne, J. Ranken. "The New Play." *Evening Post* 13 Feb. 1920.

Praises *He and She* for its courageous presentation of an insoluble problem, but finds its vision too pessimistic. Praises the conventional characters of the play more than the rebellious ones, finding them closer to human truths.

R137 Welsh, Robert Gilbert. "Miss Rachel Crothers as Author, Player and Producer." *Evening Telegram* 13 Feb. 1920.

While Welsh, like MacGowan, compares *He and She* to James Forbes's *The Famous Mrs. Fair*, he finds Crothers's work much more serious and successful, a fact appreciated by "one of the most distinguished audiences of the year" on opening night. He praises the play's light touch with its serious theme and predicts that its subject will be the center of "many discussions in clubs and at afternoon teas" in years to come. He also remarks on Crothers's ability to play the triple role of writer, producer and performer.

R138 Woollcott, Alexander. "The Play: Rachel Crothers, Herself." *Times* 13 Feb. 1920.

Like Welsh, Woollcott mentions the "alert and appreciative audience" which packed the Little Theatre to "witness a valiant and unusual undertaking" as Crothers performed in the play she wrote. While he praises her understanding and intelligence in the role, however, he also mentions her "obvious inexpertness." In a rather discursive review he praises Crothers's attempts with her serious subject in *He and She* but finds the play "not quite conclusive."

1921-1930

1921-1922

R139 Baker, Colgate. "Rachel Crothers and 'Everyday' a Dramatic Delight." *The Review* 26 Nov. 1921.

In an extended article Baker praises Crothers for her ability to "make flappers flap" in her sophisticated comedies. He quotes Crothers as saying she "wanted to picture a thoroughly modern intellectual girl of the highest ideals" who is saved from making the "fatal mistake" of marrying for convention rather than for love.

R140 Benchly, Robert. "Nice People." *Life* 24 March 1921:428.
Benchly is ambivalent about the play, wondering why one can be
wicked in any costume but in order to be virtuous one must "get a pair of
overalls and go to the country." He finds the play amusing but a bit
overdone: country people are "whiter than hyssop," while "the urban
population is uniformly and individually wicked." He theorizes that this
accounts for the "overwhelming drift from rural districts into the cities."

R141 Dale, Alan. "'Everyday' Tells Story of Money and Power." *American* 17
Nov. 1921.
Finds the play a bit overdone, too heavily freighted with a "message
for humanity," but praises the acting.

R142 Dale, Alan. "Klaw Theatre Opens With 'Nice People.'" *American* 3
March 1921.
Dale is particularly enthusiastic about Francine Larrimore in her first
starring role, "with a play containing five men, four of whom offered to
marry her." He finds the play too earnest, however, with too much
moralizing and too much of the "nice black crepe de chine aunt" about it.

R143 Darnton, Charles. "'Nice People' Hits Rich Rowdies." *Evening World* 3
March 1921.
Calls Crothers an intelligent, engaging playwright but finds a "too
sensational view of Park Avenue existence" in this effort. The brand-
new Klaw Theatre, however, is pronounced a gem.

R144 DeFoe, Louis V. "Miss Crothers's Rhinestone Play." *World* 17 Nov.
1921.
Calls *Everyday* an ordinary, trite story concealed by too much
distracting stage business, a glittering rhinestone in a brass setting,
ultimately hollow.

R145 Dorsey, Earle. "Rachel Crothers and the Aspects of Her Writing."
Washington Herald 4 Dec. 1922.
In an attack on the social extravaganza of the Washington opening of
Everyday, Dorsey complains about the "evening-gowned and dinner-
jacketed" audience, the "society-girl actress" Tallulah Bankhead, and
most of all about Crothers's willingness to write for such a frivolous
audience. Although a crowd-pleaser she is "anything but a thinker or an
artist," he concludes.

R146 "Dr. Wise Denounces Lipstick and Wine." *Times* 21 March 1921:13.
A well-known rabbi uses *Nice People* as his starting point in a
sermon condemning the lewd behavior and scandalous attire of the post-
World War I generation, endorsing Crothers's message in the play.

R147 "Everyday." *Vogue* Jan. 1922.
   Says the beginning of the play promises a return to Crothers's "older and fresher and more uncompromising outlook on life and drama," but this promise is spoiled by a return to the same kind of "spineless and ill-directed situations which marred 'Nice People.'"

R148 "'Every Day' at the Bijou." *Telegram* 17 Nov. 1921.
   Praises the play for its outstanding originality and strong realism, comparing its heroine favorably to Nora in Ibsen's *A Doll's House.*

R149 "'Everyday' Gets Enthusiastic Welcome." *Journal* 17 Nov. 1921.
   Praises Crothers's writing, casting and staging of a fine play.

R150 "Francine Larrimore in the Rachel Crothers Comedy, 'Nice People,' Opens the Klaw Theatre." *Sun* 3 March 1921.
   Compares the play to a French study of young sophisticates in 1894 in its examination of "highly sexed bachelor maids" whose hectic life of smoking, drinking and flirting appalls their elders. Finds the play disappointing after a promising start because "Miss Crothers lost her courage and turned realism into sugar coated romanticism."

R151 "Klaw Theatre Opens with Big Hit." *Evening Journal* 3 March 1921.
   Unqualified praise for the winning combination of the new theater, new play, and the return to stardom of Francine Larrimore in *Nice People.*

R152 Leslie, Amy. "Rachel Crothers's Brilliant New Play." *Daily News* 3 March 1921.
   Applauds Crothers for wielding "the whip of truth" in a brilliant, stinging commentary on the modern manners of "nice people."

I153 "Looks to Stage to Mend Present Day Morals." *Herald* 24 April 1921.
   An illustrated two-page article and interview quotes Crothers as attempting, in *Nice People*, to fulfill the dramatist's duty to take "not merely a high moral tone but a decent one" in an age of frivolity. New York must set an example, Crothers says, because the influence of Broadway spreads so far. She urges girls to be independent, self-sufficient and serious, contending that, because of the War, "boys are more satisfactory than girls" in their awareness of the harsh realities of the present age.

R154 Mantle, Burns. "'Nice People' at the Klaw." *Mail* 3 March 1921.
   Calls the play one of the outstanding hits of the season, combining a serious story with light comedy, an interesting, splendidly acted effort, although cynics might scorn its earnest moral tone. The casting is praised, with Tallulah Bankhead and Francine Larrimore singled out for special attention.

R155 "Marc Klaw's New Theatre Dedicated With 'Nice People.'" *Herald* 3 March 1921.
    Finds the theater impressive, the play only acceptable, with the sin more entertaining than the virtue.

R156 "Miss Crothers Writes Her Best." *Atlantic City Gazette* 28 Oct. 1921.
    Declares that *Everyday* is in the tradition of the late Ibsen in its hard-hitting attack on smugness and self-righteousness. Praises the acting, especially Tallulah Bankhead in the starring role.

R157 "Nice People." *The Bookman* May 1921:275.
    Complains about Crothers's new entry in a string of "poppycock dramas" which are "one of the most depressing phenomena in the American theatre," failing to be either charming or entertaining but rather a "cruel and banal invention of her very own." The reviewer then predicts that it will play to "standing room every night, of course."

R158 "Nice People." *Everybody's Magazine* Nov. 1921:87-94.
    Calls *Nice People* the most interesting contribution to the argument currently raging over the behavior of modern youth, finding it both a delightful comedy of manners and serious food for thought.

R159 "Nice People." *Theatre Magazine* July 1921:16, 20-24.
    Mainly a summary of the play, the review also praises it for its courage in presenting a serious modern problem.

R160 "'Nice People' Given at the Opening of New Klaw." *Tribune* 3 March 1921.
    Praises the play for the effectiveness with which its moral message is delivered.

R161 "'Nice People' in New Theatre." *Evening Telegram* 3 March 1921.
    Praises Crothers's keen eye for the significant nuances of modern misbehavior.

R162 "'Nice People' is a Real Delight." *Zits Weekly Newspaper* 12 March 1921.
    Calls this the best play of Crothers's "illustrious career," praising its biting sarcasm and sweet, beautiful story.

R163 "'Nice People' Seen at Ford's." *Baltimore Sun* 11 Jan. 1921.
    High praise for the play's message and its acting.

R164 "Smart Play, Smart Cast, Smart People." *Christian Science Monitor* 11 Jan. 1921.
    Finds *Nice People* uneven in its presentation of contemporary

morality but sees it as a significant contribution to the debate on these morals. Refers to a recent symposium conducted by the *Atlantic Monthly* on the subject, saying the play adds insight to the argument.

R165 "Tallulah Bankhead in 'Everyday' Premiere." *Journal of Commerce* 18 Nov. 1921.

Hails the arrival of Bankhead as a new star in a play which is effective and enjoyable.

R166 Towne, J. Ranken. "The Play." *Post* 17 Nov. 1921.

Praises the intellectual strength of *Everyday*, calling it a play of great interest and much possibility.

R167 Whittaker, James. "'Everyday's' Two Chief Characters Never Do Appear." *News* 17 Nov. 1921.

Finds Crothers resorting to formula writing and dodging the issues she brings up. Part of the problem, he says, is that she makes all the characters unlikable, so the audience has no one to sympathize with.

R168 Whittaker, James. "'Nice People' Has Bitter Truth In It And Is Great." *News* 3 March 1921.

Finds skillful presentation of acid truth in a great modern comedy.

R169 Woollcott, Alexander. "The Play: 'Everyday.'" *Times* 17 Nov. 1921.

Finds the play only a "fair-to-middling" comedy, but praises the effective cast. Predicts success but concludes that it is not "a good enough play to get excited about."

R170 Woollcott, Alexander. "The Play: The Severe Miss Crothers." *Times* 3 March 1921.

Calls *Nice People* "pointed and genuinely interesting" but somewhat disappointing because of an unsatisfying "threadbare" conclusion.

1923

R171 "At the 39th Street Theatre, 'Mary the 3d.'" *World* 6 Feb. 1923.

Despite a promising beginning the play does not succeed because of an ending in which the author "lost her nerve." The play reveals nothing really new about modern marriage.

R172 Darnton, Charles. "Mary the 3rd Presents Fine Actors." *Evening World* 6 Feb. 1923.

Praises the cast and acting but finds the message of the play unpleasant, disliking the trial marriage plot and the strained happy ending.

R173 Dimmick, Ruth Crosby. "The Theater." *Telegraph* 6 Feb. 1923.
Finds high praise for *Mary the 3rd*, especially its entertaining yet perceptive presentation of modern marriage.

I174 Lowry, Helen Bullitt. "They Stage the Modern Woman." *Pictorial Review* April 1923:50+.
A long, chatty profile of four modern woman dramatists, Crothers, Susan Glaspell, Clare Kummer and Zoe Akins, emphasizing their modernity, feminism and independence. Crothers's strength as playwright-director, and the rarity of women who perform that dual function, is emphasized. Crothers is also quoted on the difficulty of finding men who will accept intellectual and creative women on their own terms.

R175 "Mary the 3rd." *Globe* 6 Feb. 1923.
Finds this Crothers's most effective play to date, although it does find fault with unnatural dialogue.

R176 "Mary the 3rd." *Journal* 6 Feb. 1923.
Treats both Crothers and the play very seriously, finding the play solid and significant and quoting Crothers extensively on the morals and attitudes of modern young people.

R177 "Mary the 3d." *Theatre Magazine* April 1923:20.
This review is rather condescending about Crothers's "discovery" of free love, finding her "hopelessly old-fashioned" and ultimately rather cruel in her presentation of the young people's view of their parents' marriage. It concludes that Crothers has "contributed nothing of importance to current drama" in this "cumbersome" play.

R178 "Mary the 3d Interests." *Times* 6 Feb. 1923.
Despite some questioning of the philosophical pretensions of the play the review calls it one of the best Crothers has written. It does, however, question the breadth of her attack on "marriage and nearly everything connected with it," finding that the attack is weakened by including too much in its scope.

R179 "'Mary the 3d,' Newest Play by Rachel Crothers Pleases at the Court Square." *Springfield* (Ill.) *Daily News* 26 Jan. 1923.
While finding the play a bit repetitious and discursive the review calls it "daring and original," rivaled only by the modernism of Bernard Shaw in its attack on conventional attitudes.

R180 "'Mary the 3d' Unusual Play." *Springfield,* (Ill.) *Daily Republican* 26 Jan. 1923.
Calls the play an answer to the theatrical drought which has plagued Springfield, praising the mixture of comic touches and serious themes.

R181 "The New Play." *Telegram* 6 Feb. 1923.
Finds the play wholesome and entertaining, not at all offensive despite its playful look at a potentially serious subject.

I182 Snyder, Ruth. "'Mothers, Know Your Own Daughters!' Is Lesson Taught by Rachel Crothers." *Journal* 18 Feb. 1923:8.
An extensive interview on the moral dimensions of *Mary the 3rd*, emphasizing Crothers's strong sense of honesty and her approval of the younger generation which refuses to accept their parents' opinions without testing them. Crothers is quoted at length.

R183 "39th Street Theater." *Brooklyn Times* 8 Feb. 1923.
Praises the play's acting and its overall effect, but criticizes Crothers for having too negative an attitude toward marriage.

1924

R184 Broun, Heywood. "The New Play." *World* 17 April 1924.
Calls *Expressing Willie* one of the best plays of the season and "among the most skillful of American comedies."

R185 Corbin, John. "Rachel Crothers Triumphs." *Times* 17 April 1924.
Saying that "a very wonderful thing happened last night," Corbin praises every aspect of *Expressing Willie*, especially its light, satiric comedy.

R186 "Mr. Hornblow Goes to the Play: 'Expressing Willie.'" *Theatre Magazine* June 1924.
Praises the "clever and hilarious" situations, the unusually witty dialogue and the admirable casting, acting and direction, concluding that the Equity Players are fortunate to have added Crothers to their repertory. Predicts that it will be "one of the biggest hits of the season."

R187 Osborn, E.W. "Gossip From Stage: The New Play." *Evening World* 26 May 1924.
High praise for the "hilarious comedy" which provides "sixty seconds of delight" for every minute in "Expressing Willie."

R188 Welsh, Robert Gilbert. "Willie and His Week-End." *Evening Telegram* 26 May 1924.
Praises the Equity Players for saving this, their best production, until the end of their season, thereby "astonishing New York with a real American comedy." The play is praised for handling its theme "lightly and brilliantly."

R189 "'Willie' Expresses Himself Anew." *Telegram and Evening Mail* 26 May 1924.

In a combined feature, review and interview with the actor playing the lead role, both the effective comedy and the brilliant acting of the play are praised.

R190 Woollcott, Alexander. "Rachel Crothers Outdoes Herself." *Sun* 17 April 1924.

Praises *Expressing Willie* not only on its own merits as a witty, observant contemporary comedy, but also for its "rescue" of the Equity Players, who had been "floundering" until this hit.

1925-1926

R191 Dale, Alan. "Rachel Crothers's Comedy Features Two Nash Sisters." *American* 24 Nov. 1925.

The acting of the Nash sisters, "nice, nasal and nifty," is praised but *A Lady's Virtue* is called "somewhat desperate," and "missionary." Crothers "always feels and always says that men are not quite nice," Dale concludes, while still finding the play amusing.

R192 Hammond, Percy. "The Theaters." *Herald Tribune* 24 Nov. 1925.

Praises the material and the quality of the acting in *A Lady's Virtue*, but finds the plot too implausible for real effectiveness.

R193 "'A Lady's Virtue' is a Pleasing Drama." *Times* 24 Nov. 1925.

Calls the play enjoyable, clever, smooth and graceful despite a somewhat trite plot. The acting is especially praised.

R194 "Mr. Hornblow Goes to the Play: 'A Lady's Virtue.'" *Theatre Magazine* Feb. 1926:16.

Praises Crothers's "unerring instinct" for theatre in a play which, while occasionally melodramatic or mawkish, on the whole provides a diverting and entertaining evening.

R195 Rathbun, Stephen. "Nash Sisters Are Co-Stars in 'A Lady's Virtue.'" *Sun* 24 Nov. 1925.

While noting that the play conforms to Crothers's "usual formula-- sophisticated action and dialogue for two acts, with a throwback to conventional morality in the last act," Rathbun predicts the play will be a success.

1927

R196 "'A Little Journey' Comes to the Capitol Theater." *Herald-Tribune* 2 Jan. 1927.

The review of the filmed version of Crothers's play is praised for its entertaining and romantic story, but the reviewer objects to its leaving so much of the play's plot behind.

R197   Atkinson, Brooks. "The Play: Toward a Millennium." *Times* 27 Dec. 1927.
Finding *Venus* a compete failure, Atkinson concludes that Crothers has put together an unimaginative play on an "uncommonly imaginative theme."

R198   "Haines Plays Gallantly as Lover in 'A Little Journey.'" *Graphic* 3 Jan. 1927.
Finds the film pleasantly entertaining, with effective acting and an amusing plot.

R199   Smith, Alison. "The New Play: Astronomical." *World* 26 Dec. 1927.
While calling Crothers "generally lucid and successful" as a playwright, Smith finds *Venus* an unqualified disaster, "so delirious in its crazy-quilt design as to baffle all attempts" at comprehension, an unintelligible, unpleasant effort.

R200   Watts, Richard. "'Venus,' New Comedy by Rachel Crothers, in Preview Offering." *Herald Tribune* 22 Dec.1927.
Like the rest of the critics, Watts disliked *Venus* intensely. Concluding that Crothers had exhausted herself so thoroughly in arriving at her fantastic idea that she had no energy left for playwriting skill, he finds it "unappetizing and unintelligent."

1929

R201   Atkinson, J. Brooks. "The Plays." *Times* 22 Feb. 1929.
Praises *Let Us Be Gay* for moving "with a directness that verges dangerously on abruptness" but never goes too far. Praises the directing and acting but finds the plot a bit slight.

R202   Ervine, St. John. "The New Play." *World* 22 Feb. 1929.
Praises *Let Us Be Gay* as a genuine comedy of manners, finding the dialogue and the development of ideas especially full of comic enjoyment and "spontaneous fun."

R203   Gabriel, Gilbert. "Miss Larrimore in Crothers Comedy of Much Delight." *American* 22 Feb. 1929.
Announcing that Crothers has "redeemed herself" after writing *Venus*, "that strange, wretched fantasy of hers which blighted Christmas night a season ago," Gabriel praises *Let Us Be Gay* as a "smart, happy, witty" play.

R204 Hammond, Percy. "The Theaters." *Herald Tribune* 22 Feb. 1929.
  Finds *Let Us Be Gay* "one of the most amusing festivals of its kind," praising its "hornet humor" and the general effectiveness of the social observation.

R205 Littel, Robert. "Let Us Be Gay." *Theatre Arts Monthly*. March 1929;
  Calls this one of the best comedies of the season, praising Crothers's direction and the acting of the entire cast. The presentation of modern attitudes toward marriage is also praised.

R206 Lockridge, Richard. "Let Us Be Gay." *Sun* 22 Feb. 1929.
  Praises the excellent direction and acting in this "civilized, sophisticated, realistic" comedy.

R207 Pollock, Arthur. "Plays and Things." *Brooklyn Eagle* 26 Feb. 1929.
  Proclaiming this "another lucky week for the theater," Pollock calls *Let Us Be Gay* "heaven sent," finding it smart, sophisticated, sure to please any taste. It is a "jolly, wise, contemporary" comedy which could not possibly offend anyone.

R208 Van Doren, Mark. "The Drama." *The Nation* 25 March 1929:338.
  Predicts inevitable success for *Let Us Be Gay*, calling it clever, clear and intelligent. The success will be ephemeral, however, Van Doren predicts, judging that Crothers "needs a dash of madness" along with her wisdom in order to endure.

1930

I209 Steell, Willis. "American Playwright Will Direct in Paris Her Translated Play." *Herald* (Paris ed.) 23 March 1930.
  An interview with Crothers, in Paris to direct a translation of *Mary the 3rd*, emphasizing her independence and strong-mindedness as a director, a field entirely dominated by men.

R210 Tarbell, Ida M. "Fifty Foremost Women of United States Listed by Ida Tarbell." *Los Angeles Times* 14 Sept. 1930.
  Among a list of such distinguished women as Gertrude Vanderbilt, Willa Cather, Edith Wharton and Edna St. Vincent Millay, Crothers is chosen as one of the outstanding women of the American theater not only on the strength of her plays themselves, but also because of her success as a director.

1931-1939

1931

R211   Adams, Mildred. "Rachel Crothers, Playmaker." *The Woman's Journal* May 1931:11, 38, 39.

In a substantial article on the occasion of the opening of *As Husbands Go*, Adams presents Crothers as a pioneer among women in the theater, a power in a field historically hostile to women as directors and managers. Adams calls Crothers's reputation "unique" in that she is creative, a moneymaker and a craftsman all at the same time. She quotes Crothers on the subject of her self-described "Comedie Humaine de la Femme," a cycle of plays which "expressed play by play the social attitude toward women which was current at the time of the writing, and which taken as a whole mirrored women's progress" in the century.

R212   Atkinson, J. Brooks. "Miss Crothers at Her Best." *Times* 6 March 1931.

Mentioning the length of Crothers's career (25 years) and the durability of her popularity, Atkinson marvels at her ability to keep topping herself. He especially praises *As Husbands Go* for its "abundant sympathy with ordinary people," its comedy and its "depth of heart-breaking emotion."

R213   Atkinson, J. Brooks. "The Theatrical Season: Not So Bad As Some." *Times* 15 March 1931.

In an overview article for the Sunday edition Atkinson considers the 1931 season as a whole, finding it unusually distinguished. Special praise is reserved for Noel Coward's *Private Lives* and Crothers's *As Husbands Go*.

R214   Barnes, Djuna. "The Tireless Rachel Crothers." *Theatre Guild Magazine* May 1931:17-18.

In a biographical article Barnes quotes Crothers on her debts to three women to whom she "owes [her] freedom"--actress Carlotta Nilsson, Mrs. Wheatcroft, who started her in directing, and actress Maxine Elliott, who helped establish her reputation. Crothers is quoted as finding women "more daring," more willing to take chances in the theater, than men.

R215   Brown, John Mason. "The New Plays." *Evening Post.* 6 March 1931.

Calls *As Husbands Go* one of the best plays of the season, praising the play's comedy and its infectious appeal to the audience, which enjoyed it immensely.

R216   Budd, Dorothy. "When You Are Forty-Six." *Woman's Home Companion* Aug. 1931:71.

Crothers discusses clothing, both personal and theatrical, in an article emphasizing the skill with which she has used costume to develop character and create effects in all her plays.

R217 "Crothers Play is 'Repeat.'" *Morning Telegraph* 15 March 1931.
Like Atkinson, this reviewer is struck by the number of Crothers's successes, calling *As Husbands Go* a repeat of her former triumphs and praising her for 23 productions which were never less than admirably professional.

I218 Forman, Henry James. "The Story of Rachel Crothers, America's Leading Woman Playwright." *Pictorial Review* June 1931:2, 56, 59.
An effusive personality portrait which is as eager to reassure its readers that Crothers is not strenuously feminist as it is to describe her success.

R219 Gabriel, Gilbert. "'As Husbands Go,' Rachel Crothers's Newest & Heartiest Comedy, All Sorts of a Treat." *American* 15 March 1931.
Gabriel finds the play somewhat "loose-jointed and uneven," but praises it as "heartily native and natural," a thoroughly enjoyable play.

R220 Garland, Robert. "Rachel Crothers's Comedy Clean and Full of Humor." *World-Telegram* 6 March 1931.
Garland calls *As Husbands Go* good news for Broadway, praising Crothers, John Golden as producer, and even the "eighteen-karat audience" which fully appreciated this "smart, sappy, funny" comedy. The acting and direction are especially strongly praised, though the story is acknowledged to be slight.

R221 Garland, Robert. "The Theaters." *World-Telegram* 5 Nov. 1931.
While Garland is kinder than most of the critics, he too finds *Caught Wet* unsatisfying, unconvincing and not up to Crothers's usual high standards.

R222 Hammond, Percy. "Caught Wet." *Herald-Tribune* 5 Nov. 1931.
While describing himself as a fan of Crothers's work, the reviewer finds the play unsatisfying, falling far short of her usual accomplishments.

R223 Hutchens, John. "That Times Square Veteran, Rachel Crothers." *Times* 15 March 1931.
An overview of Crothers's 25-year career, emphasizing both her personal qualities and her consistent level of professionalism as a "Broadway veteran."

R224 Lockridge, Richard. "Caught Wet." *Sun* 5 Nov. 1931.
Finds the play far from Crothers's usual high standards of excellence, finding it a "parlor game" by someone who is wasting her talent.

I225 McCarroll, Marion Clyde. "Directing a Play Is Like Leading an Orchestra, Says Rachel Crothers, Rehearsing Her 23rd Production." *Evening Post* 4 March 1931.

In an interview/feature article McCarroll concentrates on Crothers as director, a playwright who has refused the traditional role of standing "sadly by while an iron-willed director manhandles the lines and the players as he pleases." Crothers is praised for her versatility and professionalism.

R226 McLaughlin, Russell. "A Fine Comedy at the Wilson." *Detroit News* 30 Nov. 1931.

"Hard times or no hard times, this is the play to see," pronounces McLaughlin, calling *As Husbands Go* a must even for those who can afford only one play this season.

I227 Phillips, Henry Albert. "The Theater, Its Plays and Its People: Rachel Crothers Talks of Her Plays." *Herald Tribune* 15 March 1931.

An interview providing an overview of Crothers's career, especially emphasizing her intention to present a "cycle of women and sex," what she terms a "Comedie Humaine de la Femme," in her early plays. The strength of her commitment to dramatic excellence and artistic integrity is clear in her lengthy comments to Phillips.

R228 "Prominent Women Take Seats for 'As Husbands Go.'" *Evening Post* 4 March 1931.

The social significance of a Crothers play is indicated by this long list of socialites who attended a pre-opening performance to benefit the Professional Children's School.

R229 Ruhl, Arthur. "'As Husbands Go,' Crothers Play, Presented at the John Golden." *Herald* 6 March 1931.

Calling the play "first-class entertainment, made out of sound American stuff," Ruhl praises the satiric humor, the perceptive observation of American character types, the acting and the delightful plot.

R230 "Second Looks at Broadway." *Herald-Tribune* 7 May 1931.

Finds *As Husbands Go* worthy of a Pulitzer Prize in a second review of a play deemed worthy of a visit even during the coming summer heat.

R231 Shaw, Len G. "The Theatre." *Detroit Free Press* 30 Nov. 1931.

While Rachel Crothers exists there is hope for the future of articulate drama, Shaw contends, praising *As Husbands Go* for its casting, its direction, and above all for the quality of the play itself.

R232 Winchell, Walter. "'As Husbands Go.' At Golden, Delightful New Comedy Hit." *Daily Mirror* 6 March 1931.
Crothers has distinguished herself again, Winchell announces, enchanting her audience with the intelligence and simplicity of her play. The acting is especially praised.

1932-1933

R233 Atkinson, Brooks. "The People and Miss Crothers." *Times* 16 Oct., 1932.
Finds *When Ladies Meet* a worthy addition to Crothers's 25-year career, calling some of the devices a bit dated but praising the social observation in the play.

R234 Atkinson, Brooks. "The Play: Two Women & One Man in a Jovial Comedy by Rachel Crothers." *Times* 7 Oct. 1932.
Suggests that *When Ladies Meet* is a bit formulaic, and certainly an unkind observation of men's foibles, but finds it an essentially agreeable, entertaining play.

R235 Brown, John Mason. "When Ladies Meet." *Evening Post* 7 Oct. 1932.
Finds that the new season has taken a turn for the better with this play, praising Crothers's writing, casting and direction.

R236 Gabriel, Gilbert. "When Ladies Meet." *American* 7 Oct. 1932
Finds the play wise, witty and entertaining, especially praising the blissfully funny Spring Byington.

R237 Garland, Robert. "'When Ladies Meet' An Instant Success at Royale Theatre." *World-Telegram* 7 Oct. 1932.
Calls this the first out-and-out success of the season, praising Crothers's durability and excellence over her amazing career. This is her best play yet, Garland concludes.

R238 Hall, Mordaunt. "Ann Harding, Frank Morgan, Alice Brady and Others in a Film Version of 'When Ladies Meet.'" In *The New York Times Film Reviews 1913-1968*. P. 953.
Calls the film witty and intelligent but finds it more talk than action. Praises the acting, especially that of Myrna Loy.

R239 Hutchens, John. "Greece to Broadway: Broadway in Review." *Theatre Arts Monthly* June 1932:24.
Calls *Caught Wet* a "great deal of pother about nothing" which attempts to satirize the bad manners of modern youth but becomes only an unsuccessful mystery drama. "It promised not to work and it didn't," Hutchens concludes.

R240 Krutch, Joseph Wood. "Drama." *The Nation* 26 Oct. 1932:408.
    Calling Crothers an "enlightened defender of conventional virtues,"
Krutch praises *When Ladies Meet* as a well-made play and an audience-
pleaser. He finds it "almost completely spoiled by its moralizing
generalities," however, relying on platitudes instead of real moral vision.
He does praise Spring Byington's comedy, finding her sly revelations
more truly moral than the rest of the play.

R241 Lockridge, Richard. "When Ladies Meet." *Sun* 7 Oct. 1932.
    Says the play "comes close to being the finest of all that long
procession of admirable plays" Crothers has written, concluding that its
subtle, compassionate tone adds dignity to the Broadway season. He
especially praises the "brilliant" casting.

R242 Mantle, Burns. "'When Ladies Meet' Is a Comedy Hit." *Daily News* 7
    Oct. 1932.
    Calls this the first real comedy hit of the season, especially praising
Crothers's casting and direction.

R243 Mears, Marjorie. "All Counterfeit Curios Vanish When Miss Crothers
    Stages Play." *Herald Tribune* 1 Nov. 1932.
    In a behind-the-scenes feature for the Sunday edition, Mears follows
Crothers as she shops New York for appropriate props and costumes,
praising her perfectionism in creating exactly the right "look" for each of
her plays.

R244 Morgan, Charles. "Meeting in London." *Times* 14 May 1933.
    Reviewing *When Ladies Meet* on tour in London, Morgan is dubious
about the formulaic exactness with which Crothers makes her points, but
concludes that she can get away with anything--it's a hit in London as it
was in New York.

R245 "Pleasing Revival at Forrest Theater." *American* 20 Jan. 1933.
    Praises the revival of *As Husbands Go* as a worthwhile addition to
the season's dramatic offerings.

R246 "Rachel Crothers, Pacemaker for American Social Comedy." *Theatre
    Arts Monthly* Dec. 1932:971-72.
    Credits Crothers with covering the last quarter-century more
thoroughly and perceptively than any other American playwright,
providing a "vigorous record" of the time.

R247 Ruhl, Arthur. "The Theater: 'When Ladies Meet.'" *Herald Tribune* 7 Oct.
    1932.
    In an extremely enthusiastic review Ruhl praises the play, the
casting, the acting, even the sets. Crothers's "countrymen are in her
debt" for the play, he concludes.

1936-1938

R248   Anderson, John. "'Susan and God' Shows Suave Craftsmanship." *Journal-American* 8 Oct. 1937.

Anderson is pleased to welcome Crothers back "from the Lotos-Land of Hollywood" and says the audience loved the play, but he finds it only partially satisfactory, "jittery and unrestrained." Susan, despite Gertrude Lawrence's magnificent performance, is "a fool."

R249   Brown, John Mason. "Gertrude Lawrence Seen as the Star of 'Susan and God.'" *Evening Post* 8 Oct. 1937.

Finds Crothers a dependable, interesting, intelligent playwright, always able to turn out a well-made play of ideas. The play is an interesting portrait of a charming but essentially selfish character, admirably portrayed by Lawrence.

R250   Flexner, Eleanor. "Rachel Crothers." In *American Playwrights 1918-1938: The Theatre Retreats From Reality.* New York: Simon & Schuster, 1938.

Praises Crothers's ability to keep up with rapidly-changing times but contends that her first work was stronger and more effective than her later plays. Discusses her social ideas, especially her feminism, in detail, finding her becoming more conservative than progressive after World War I.

R251   Isaacs, Edith. "Susan and God." *Theatre Arts Monthly* Dec. 1937:918-19.

While not necessarily the best of Crothers's efforts the play is an interesting, observant comedy of manners revealing a great deal about wishful thinking and self-indulgence, Isaacs concludes. She commends Crothers's wisdom and craftsmanship as well as Gertrude Lawrence's fine performance.

R252   Krutch, Joseph Wood. "Religion in the Drawing-room." *The Nation* 23 Oct. 1937:455-57.

Finds *Susan and God* witty and observant of modern fads, but intellectually weak and, though likely to be a hit, ultimately unsatisfying.

R253   Lockridge, Richard. "The New Plays: 'Susan and God,' With Gertrude Lawrence, Opens at the Plymouth Friday." *Sun* 8 Oct. 1937.

Lockridge states that producer John Golden and playwright Rachel Crothers, aided by "a Gertrude Lawrence all animation and high jinks, brightened the season considerably" with this "slight and somewhat confused frolic." He concludes that the play doesn't really make sense, but that it's so much fun it doesn't matter.

R254 Mantle, Burns. "Susan and God." *Daily News* 8 Oct. 1937.

      Calls this another worthwhile addition to the season, a domestic comedy marked by astute observation and great common sense. Like the rest of the critics, Mantle is struck by Lawrence's performance, calling her "radiant" in the title role.

R255 Quinn, Arthur Hobson. "Rachel Crothers and the Feminine Criticism of Life." In *A History of the American Drama From the Civil War to the Present Day*. Vol. II. Rev. ed. New York: Appleton-Century-Crofts, 1936. Rpt. Irving Publishers, Inc., 1979.

      An extensive survey of Crothers's career and her ideas, rejecting the labels "conventional and conservative" and finding her a major force in twentieth century drama.

R256 Vernon, Grenville. "Susan and God." *The Commonweal* 22 Oct. 1937:606.

      While finding the play "not a supreme piece of comic writing," Vernon praises Crothers for presenting "moral virtues which mean something. She never turns the basic virtues on their heads and labels them vices," he says, and calls this "the most delightful play" of the season.

R257 Watts, Richard. "The Theaters: 'Susan and God.'" *Herald Tribune* 8 Oct. 1937.

      Watts praises the dialogue and characterization of the play but finds it essentially unsatisfying. Underneath the sparkling surface, he says, the heroine is unlikable. Nevertheless he finds Lawrence "ravishing" in the lead role.

1939

R258 Brown, John Mason. "Two on the Aisle: Honoring the Theatre and Rachel Crothers." *Post* 19 April 1939.

      The transcript of an address by Brown at the White House on the occasion of Crothers's receiving the Chi Omega National Achievement Award for 1938. Crothers was only the second person from the theater to win the award, the first having been Katharine Cornell.

1940-1958

B259 Abrahamson, Irving I. "The Career of Rachel Crothers in the American Theater." Ph.D. Dissertation, University of Chicago, 1956.

      An overview of Crothers's life and career emphasizing her modernism, her feminism and her substantial contributions to twentieth century drama.

I260 Bugbee, Emma. "Rachel Crothers Feels the Urge to Write a Play This Summer." *Herald-Tribune* 21 April 1941.

In a lengthy interview Bugbee describes Crothers's numerous activities as founder and president of the American Theatre Wing Allied Relief Fund, and her intention to try to write a new play soon. Crothers is quoted as saying she is unsure if she will "ever write another play," however, questioning whether it is "important" that she should, in a time of war.

R261 Crowther, Bosley. "When Ladies Meet." In *The New York Times Film Reviews 1913-1968*, p. 1410.

The 1941 film of Crothers's play is dismissed as a dated, "Hoover-vintage" waste of effort, trying too hard to be amusing, and failing even to be interesting.

B262 Gagey, Edmond M. "Comedy--American Plan." In *Revolution in American Drama*. New York: Columbia University Press, 1947.

Considers Crothers's ability to be both daring and commercial, developing "problem dramas" over several decades without losing her large popular audience. While he finds fault with her tendency to play it safe, he praises her technical skill and her acute social observation.

B263 Hughes, Charlotte. "Women Play-Makers." *The New York Times Magazine* 4 May 1941:10, 11, 27.

Hughes considers significant contemporary women dramatists, including Crothers along with Lillian Hellman, Clare Booth, Zoe Akins and Edna Ferber, in an article which emphasizes their independence while downplaying any suggestion of radical feminism.

I264 "Miss Rachel Crothers Busy at Two Jobs in New York City." (Bloomington, Ill.) *Pantagraph* 24 Nov. 1940.

Crothers is quoted in a letter to her sister describing her founding of the American Theatre Wing Allied Relief Fund. Josephine Hull, Gertrude Lawrence, Antoinette Perry, Theresa Hepburn and Vera Allen were chosen to help her launch the project.

1960-1990

B265 Ashton, Jean. "The Neil Simon of Her Day--And an Ardent Feminist." *Times* 25 May 1980:D8.

On the occasion of the Brooklyn Academy of Music revival of *He and She*, Ashton provides an overview of Crothers's career, defining her significance to the Broadway stage and praising the timeless relevance of her social observation, especially her "three-dimensional female characters attempting to cope with problems that have not disappeared."

B266 Block, Anita. *The Changing World in Plays and Theater*. Rpt. New York: Da Capo Press, 1971.
    In a study which emphasizes the social relevance of drama, Block criticizes Crothers as typical of commercial Broadway superficiality.

B267 Gottlieb, Lois. "The Double Standard Debate in Early 20th-Century American Drama." *The Michigan Academician* Spring 1975:441-52.
    Considers Rhy MacChesney's struggle against conventional ideas of femininity in an article developing Crothers's modernism and feminism. Finds *The Three of Us* a "radical challenge" to the commonly accepted double standard despite an ending which is more conventional than the play's earlier confrontation with tradition.

B268 Gottlieb, Lois. "Obstacles to Feminism in the Early Plays of Rachel Crothers." *University of Michigan Papers in Women's Studies* June 1975:71-84.
    Focusing on Crothers's development of the conflict between woman's need for independence and her need for love, Gottlieb finds that Crothers presents a powerfully realistic picture of an insoluble struggle to reconcile the desire for feminism and the desire for traditional femininity and love.

B269 Gottlieb, Lois. *Rachel Crothers*. Boston: Twayne Publishers, 1979.
    In the only full-length study of Crothers yet published, Gottlieb surveys her life and career, considering her strengths and weaknesses in detail. She emphasizes Crothers's modernism, her feminism, and the changes in her reputation over the course of the twentieth century.

R270 Gussow, Mel. "Theater: 'He and She' of 1911 in Brooklyn." *Times* 30 May 1980.
    Finds *He and She* not relevant in its 1980 revival.

R271 "He and She." *Variety* 4 June 1980.
    Finds the play as strong and relevant as Ibsen, praising the revival for bringing a period play to the modern public.

R272 "He and She." *Women's Wear Daily* 2 June 1980:24.
    Finds the revival startlingly contemporary, calling it a thought-provoking reminder of the slow rate of progress in women's issues.

R273 Kaplan, Zoe. "Rachel and Prejudice." *Other Stages* 12 June 1980:63.
    Reviewing the Brooklyn Academy of Music revival of *He and She*, Kaplan praises Crothers's timeliness and hard-mindedness, especially her emphasis on the need for sexual and economic equality. Stresses the strength and farsightedness of her feminism.

R274   Lawson, Steve. "Women Now and Then." *Soho Weekly News* 4 June 1980.

Finds the content of *He and She* dated, but praises the revival for its attempt at presenting historically significant American plays.

B275   Mersand, Joseph. "Rachel Crothers: First Lady Among the Dramatists." In *The Play's the Thing*. Rpt. New York: Kennikat Press, Inc., 1965.

Considers Crothers as a modernist and feminist, praising her astute social observation, the candor with which she addressed social problems, and the skill which enabled her to write successful commercial and intellectual plays over nearly half a century. Defends her against the charge of conservatism leveled against her by some critics.

R276   Moranca, Bonnie. "'He and She' at the American Theatre Co." *Show Business* 11 March 1971:19.

Reviews the production favorably, finding the play as timely and relevant to women's lives in the second half of the twentieth century as it was in the first.

R277   Munk, Erika. "A Frieze Grows in Brooklyn." *Village Voice* 9 June 1980.

Finds the revival of *He and She* a failure, calling Crothers a snob and declaring that the play trivializes the problems women face in trying to combine careers and families.

R278   Oliver, Edith. "The Theater." *The New Yorker* 9 June 1980.

In a review of the Brooklyn Academy of Music revival of *He and She*, Oliver finds the play witty, acutely observed, and not at all dated.

B279   Schlueter, June, ed. *Modern American Drama: The Female Canon.* Rutherford, N.J.: Fairleigh Dickinson University Press, 1990.

In a valuable collection of essays surveying American women dramatists of the eighteenth, nineteenth and twentieth centuries, Crothers's position as both popular writer and contributor to the feminist discourse is assessed.

B280   Shafer, Yvonne B. "The Liberated Woman in American Plays of the Past." *Players* April-May 1974:95-100.

Considers early twentieth century feminist drama by both men and women, praising Crothers's comedy, her objectivity and the accuracy of her social picture. Finds her material, with minor exceptions, undated.

R281   Simon, John. "The Theater." *New York Magazine* 16 June 1980.

Wonders why anyone bothered to revive *He and She*, finding the play conventional, manipulative and filled with cliches.

R282   Stasio, Marilyn. "Splendid 'He and She' at BAM." *Post* 30 May 1980.

Praises the revival for its startling freshness, insisting that the issues and attitudes are as contemporary as conversations overheard in New York stores.

R283 Steinberg, Saul. "'A Man's World' Revived." *Stages* March 1986.
Finds the play an interesting period piece but ultimately dated, with many stereotypes, both ethnic and sexual. Mentions the receptive and enthusiastic audience.

R284 "A Strikingly Modern Look at Feminism--in a 1910 Drama." *Christian Science Monitor* 5 June 1980:19.
Praises the effort of reviving *He and She*, finding the play as modern as films made 70 years after it was written.

B285 Sutherland, Cynthia. "American Women Playwrights as Mediators of the 'Woman Problem.'" *Modern Drama* Sept. 1978:319-36.
Sutherland traces Crothers's development from the articulate feminism of *A Man's World* to the ambivalence of the late plays, concluding that Crothers became disillusioned with "feminist causes."

R286 Watt, Douglas. "Past Yields Urgent Feminist Message." *Daily News* 30 May 1980:15.
Praises the strong feminism of the revival of *He and She* but finds the argument too didactic to be successful.

Listings in Reference Works

B287 *Columbia Literary History of the United States.* New York: Columbia University Press, 1988. P. 1103.
Mentioned only in passing as a "social satirist" who emerged "from under O'Neill's dark shadow" to write audience-pleasing comedies, Crothers is largely dismissed as a significant influence in modern drama.

B288 Edelman, Floyd E., ed. "Rachel Crothers." *American Drama Criticism: Interpretations. 1890-1977.* 2nd ed. Hamden, Conn.: The Shoestring Press, Inc., 1979. P. 30-32.
Lists sources of review of *As Husbands Go, Expressing Willie, Let Us Be Gay, A Little Journey, Susan and God* and *When Ladies Meet.*

B289 Hewitt, Barnard. "Rachel Crothers." *The Readers Encyclopedia of World Drama.* New York: Thomas Y. Crowell Co., 1969. P. 157.
Praises Crothers's skill in technical matters but finds her plays "essentially dramas of sentiment" distinguished by the smart, witty dialogue of their wealthy characters.

B290 Kunitz, Stanley, ed. "Rachel Crothers." *Twentieth Century Authors*, 1st supplement. New York: H.W. Wilson Co., 1955. P. 248.
In a brief consideration of her lengthy and successful career this

account says the question of whether her plays will endure has yet to be answered.

B291 McGovern, Edythe. "Rachel Crothers." *American Women Writers from Colonial Times to the Present.* Linda Maneiro, ed. Frederick Ungar Publishing Co., 1979. Pp. 428-30.

Considers Crothers fundamentally conservative, making only "a modest contribution to the American stage." Praises her fight against the double standard but concludes that most of her plays show women "happy in the traditional wife-mother role," sacrificing independence for love.

B292 "Rachel Crothers." *Contemporary Authors.* Vol. 113. Detroit: Gale Research Co., 1985. P. 107.

One-paragraph biographical sketch.

B293 "Rachel Crothers." *Dictionary of Literary Biography.* Vol. 7, part 1. Detroit: Gale Research Co., 1981. Pp. 134-41.

A biographical and critical essay incorporating contemporary critical responses. The essay concludes that Crothers's reputation as a "minor playwright" is perhaps justified, but that more judicious historical consideration of her ideas is needed.

B294 "Rachel Crothers." *McGraw-Hill Encyclopedia of World Drama.* Vol. I. New York: McGraw-Hill Publishing Co., 1972. Pp. 439-442.

An overview of Crothers's career focusing on her technical excellence and considering her a master of the comedy of manners who also depicted the changing roles of American women during the first half of the twentieth century.

B295 "Rachel Crothers." *Twentieth-Century Literary Criticism.* Vol. 19. Detroit: Gale Research Co., 1986. Pp. 69-87.

A biographical and critical essay with substantial excerpts from critics from 1910 to 1979, presenting a judicious view of Crothers's career and fluctuating critical reputation.

B296 Salem, James M., ed. *A Guide to Critical Reviews: Part I: American Drama.* 3rd ed. Metuchen, N.J.: The Scarecrow Press, Inc., 1984. Pp. 114-21.

A listing of opening dates, length of run and some reviews of American dramatists from 1909 to 1982.

B297 Spiller, Robert E., et al., eds. *Literary History of the United States.* 4th ed. New York: Macmillan Publishing Co., 1974. Pp. 1006, 1011.

Considers *A Man's World* Crothers's most important play, introducing a "question which was to be debated on the stage" for 25 years.

Productions and Credits

The following is a list of New York productions of Crothers's plays, including cast lists, length of run, producers and directors. The most reliable source for length of run is the invaluable *Best Plays of...* series, edited by Burns Mantle and Sherwood P. Garrison for the years 1899-1919, and by Mantle alone from 1920 on.

P1 *THE THREE OF US*

P1.1 *The Three of Us* opened 17 October 1906 at the Madison Square Theatre. Produced by Walter N. Lawrence, staged by George Foster Platt. Settings by P. Dodd Ackerman. 227 performances.
    Rhy MacChesney--Carlotta Nillson
    Stephen Townley--Frederic Truesdell
    Louis Berresford--Henry Kolker
    Clem MacChesney--John Westley
    Tweed Bix--Stanley Dark
    Lorimer Trenholm--Robert B. Keggeris
    "Sonnie" MacChesney--Master George Clarke
    Hop Wing--John Prescott
    Maggie--Eva Vincent
    Mrs. Tweed Bix--Jane Peyton
Reviews: R001, R002, R003, R004, R005, R006, I007, R008, R009, R010, R011, R012, R013, R014, R015, R016.

P2 *THE COMING OF MRS. PATRICK*

P2.1 *The Coming of Mrs. Patrick* opened 6 November 1907 at the Madison Square Theatre. Produced by Walter N. Lawrence. 13 performances.
    Mrs. Patrick--Laura Nelson Hall

Dr. Bruce--Melville Stewart
Mr. Lawton--James L. Carhart
Billy Lawton--Walter Thomas
Tom Crowell--Forrest Winant
Dudley Birmingham--Charles D. Coburn
Ellinor Lawton--Elizabeth Stewart
Nina Lawton--Millicent Edwards
Pauline Shank--Minnette Barrett
Chrissy Heath--Perla Landers
Matthews--George H. Wiseman
Maria--Lillie Eldridge
Reviews:R017, R018, R019, R020, R021.

P3 *MYSELF-BETTINA*

P3.1 *Myself-Bettina* opened 5 October 1908 at Daly's Theatre. Produced by Maxine Elliott. 32 performances after touring before the Broadway opening.
John Marshall--Julian L'Estrange
Lennox Marshall--Eric Maturin
Charlie Hope--Grant Mitchell
Ben--Thomas J. Kelly
Christine Marshall--Gertrude Berkeley
Annabelle Greenleaf--Susanne Perry
Abbie--Lois Frances Clark
Mamie Dean--Violet Fortescue
Bettina Dean--Maxine Elliott
Reviews: R022, R023, R024, R025, R026, R027, R028, R029.

P4 *A MAN'S WORLD*

P4.1 *A Man's World* opened 8 February 1910 at the Comedy Theatre. Produced by Lee and J.J. Shubert, staged by Crothers. 71 performances. It was revived with a month's production by the Meat & Potatoes Co. of New York City in December 1985.
Frances "Frank" Ware--Mary Mannering
Leonie Brune--Ruth Holt Boucicault
Clara Oakes--Helen Ormsbee
Malcolm Gaskell--Charles Richman
Fritz Bahn--John Sainpolis
Wells Trevor--Arthur Berthelet
Emile Grimeaux--Ernest Perrin
Kiddie--Mark Short
Reviews: R033, R034, R035, R036, R037, R038, R039, R040, R041, R042, R043, R044, R045, R046, R047, I048, R049.

P5 *OURSELVES*

P5.1 *Ourselves* opened at the Lyric Theatre 13 November 1913. Produced by Lee and J.J. Shubert, staged by J.C. Huffman and Crothers. 29 performances.
> Florence--Dorothy Taylor
> Harriette--Silvia Zan
> Miss Carew--Mattie Keene
> Beatrice Barrington--Jobyna Howland
> Sadie--Estelle Thebaud
> Stella--Caroline Page
> Lena--Louise Coleman
> Delia--Alma Rheinock
> Mabel--Blanche Natali
> Molly--Grace Elliston
> Mary--Grace Gardner
> Irene Barrington--Selene Johnson
> Wilson--Gertrude LeBrant
> Leever--Geoffrey C. Stein
> Joseph--Craig Miner
> Collin Ford--Stanley Dark
> Bob Barrington--Thurlow Bergen

Reviews: I053, R054, R055, R056, R057.

P6 *YOUNG WISDOM*

P6.1 *Young Wisdom* opened 5 January 1914 at the Criterion Theatre; in October 1914 it traveled to London. Produced by Joseph Brooks, staged by Robert Melton. 56 performances.
> Victoria Claffenden--Mabel Taliaferro
> Gail Claffenden--Edith Taliaferro
> Judge Claffenden--Aubrey Beattie
> Mrs. Claffenden--Mabel Bert
> Barry Claffenden--Junius Matthews
> Christopher Bruce--Hayward Ginn
> Peter Van Horn--Richard Sterling
> Max Norton--Regan Hughston

Reviews: R058, R062, R063, R064, R069, R070, R071, R072, R073, R074, R075, R076, R077, R078.

P7 *THE HEART OF PADDY WHACK*

P7.1 *The Heart of Paddy Whack* opened 23 November 1914. 25 performances. It was revived in March 1934 in honor of St. Patrick's Day.
> Michael--Stephen Davis
> Granny--Jessie Crommette
> Bridget O'Reilly--Jenny Lamont
> Miss Margaret Flinn--Maud Hosford

Mona Cairn--Edith Luckett
Dennis O'Malley--Chauncey Olcott
Squire Linnering--Charles E. Verner
Lawrie Linnering--Fleming Ward
Mr. O'Dowd--Richard Quilter
Mrs. O'Dowd--Bessie Lea Lestina
Mrs. McGinnis--Nina Seville
Mr. McGinnis--Walter Colligan
Reviews: R059, R060, R061, R065, R066, R067, R068

P8 *"OLD LADY 31"*

P8.1 *"Old Lady 31"* opened 30 October 1916 at The 39th St. Theatre; the idea was suggested by a novel by Louise Forsslund. Produced by Lee Kugel, staged by Crothers. 160 performances.

Angie--Emma Dunn
Abe--Reginald Barlow
Nancy--Vivia Ogden
Mrs. Homans--Mrs. Felix Morris
Sarah Jane--Maud Sinclair
Abigail--Anna Bates
Blossy--May Galyer
Mary--Mary Carroll
John--Stuart Sage
Samuel Darby--Louis Fierce
Mike--John B. Maher
Elizabeth--Elizabeth Leroy
Minerva--Lottie Church
Granny--Mary Davis
Reviews: R080, R081, R082, R083, R084, R085, R086, R087, R089, R090, R091, R092.

P9 *MOTHER CAREY'S CHICKENS*

P9.1 *Mother Carey's Chickens* opened 25 September 1917 at the Cort Theatre. Produced by John Golden, staged by Ralph Cummings. 39 performances. Adapted from the novel by Kate Douglas Wiggin.

Ossian Popham--Wallace Owen
Gilbert Carey--Lorin Raker
Nancy Carey--Edith Taliaferro
Mother Carey--Edith Barker
Kathleen-Doris Eaton
Peter--Charles Eaton
Cousin Ann Chadwick--Marie L. Day
Julia Carey--Mabel Acker
Mrs. Ossian Popham--Ursula Elsworth
Lallie Joy Popham--Helen Marqua

Ralph Thurston--Robert Glecker
Tom Hamilton--Thomas Carrigan
Henry Lord, Ph.D--Wilson Reynolds
Reviews: R093, R094, R095, R096, R097, R098, R100.

P10 *ONCE UPON A TIME*

P10.1 *Once Upon a Time* opened 3 December 1917 at the National Theatre in Washington and 15 April 1918 at the Fulton Theatre in New York. Produced by Cohan and Harris, staged by Crothers. 24 performances in New York.
John--Thomas Williams
Jerry--Chauncey Olcott
Annie--Elsie Lyding
Lizzie--Jessie Ralph
Patsy--Bonnie Marie
The Boy--George Brennan
Mary--Ethel Wilson
Jack--Edward Fielding
Lenox--W.L. Romaine
Reviews: R102, R103, R105, R110.

P11 *A LITTLE JOURNEY*

P11.1 *A Little Journey* opened at The Little Theatre 26 December 1918. Produced by Lee and J.J. Shubert, staged by Crothers. 252 performances.
Julie Rutherford--Estelle Winwood
Jim West--Cyril Keightley
Mrs. Welch--Jobyna Howland
Mrs. Bay--May Galyer
Lily--Nancy Winston
Leo Stern--Paul Burns
Frank--Victor LaSalle
Charles--Theodore Westerman, Jr.
Alfred Bemis--Edward Lester
Smith--William A. Mortimer
Annie--Gilda Verasi
Ethel--Vera Fuller-Mellish
Kittie Van Dyck--Elma Royton
The Porter--Richard Quilter
1st Conductor--George Hadden
2nd Conductor--John Robb
Reviews: R101, R104, R106, R107, R108, R109, R110, R119, R196, R198.

P12 *39 EAST*

P12.1 *39 East* opened 31 March 1919 at the Broadhurst Theatre; it moved to the Maxine Elliott Theatre on 14 July 1919. Produced by Lee and J.J. Shubert, staged by Crothers. 160 performances.

Napoleon Gibbs--Henry Hull
Count Gionelli--Luis Alberni
Timothy O'Brien--Victor Sutherland
Washington--John Kirkpatrick
Dr. Hubbard--Albert Carroll
The Policeman--John Morris
Penelope Penn--Constance Binney
Madame deMailly--Alison Skipworth
Miss MacMasters--Blanche Frederici
Mrs. Smith--Lucia Moore
Miss Sadie Clarence--Edith Gresham
Miss Myrtle Clarence--Mildred Arden
Evalina--Jessie Graham
Rosa--Gertrude Clements

Reviews: R112, R113,R114, R115, R116, R117, R118, R120, R121, R122, R123.

P13 *HE AND SHE*

P13.1 *He and She* opened 12 February 1920 at the Little Theater. Produced by Lee and J.J. Shubert, sets by Norman Bel Geddes. 28 performances.

Tom Herford--Cyril Keightley
Ann Herford--Rachel Crothers
Daisy Herford--Margaret Johnson
Millicent Herford--Faire Binney
Dr. Remington--Arthur Johnson
Keith McKenzie--Fleming Ward
Ruth Creel--Ethel Cozzens
Ellen--Frances Bryant

Reviews: R124, R125, R126, R127, R128, R129, R130, R131, R132, R133, R134, R135, R136, R137, R138.

P13.2 The cast of the 1980 revival at the Brooklyn Academy of Music included Laurie Kennedy as Ann, Gerry Bamman as Tom, and Marti Maraden, Richard Jamisen, Joan Pape, Jerome Dempsey, Cherry Jones and Helen Harrelsen. Directed by Emily Mann, lighting by William Mentzer.

Reviews: R270, R271, R272, R273, R274, R276, R277, R278, R281, R282, R283, R284, R286.

P14 *NICE PEOPLE*

P14.1 *Nice People* opened 2 March 1921 at the Klaw Theatre. Produced by Sam H. Harris, staged by Crothers. 242 performances. It was chosen one of the Best Plays of 1920-21 by Burns Mantle.

Hallie Livingston--Tallulah Bankhead
Eileen Baxter-Jones--Katharine Cornell

Trevor Leeds--Edwin Hensley
Theodora Gloucester--Francine Larrimore
Oliver Comstock--Guy Milham
Scotty Wilbur--Hugh Huntley
Margaret Rainsford--Merle Maddern
Hubert Gloucester--Frederick Perry
Billy Wade--Robert Ames
Mr. Heyfer--Frederick Maynard
Reviews: R140, R142, R143, R146, R150, R151, R152, R153, R154, R155, R157, R158, R159, R160, R161, R162, R163, R164, R168, R170.

P15 *EVERYDAY*

P15.1 *Everyday* opened 16 November 1921 at the Bijou Theatre. Produced by Mary Kirkpatrick, staged by Crothers. 30 performances. It was chosen one of the Best Plays of 1921 by Burns Mantle.
Judge Nolan--Frank Sheridan
Fannie Nolan--Minnie Dupree
Phyllis Nolan--Tallulah Bankhead
Mrs. Raymond--Lucille Watson
May Raymond--Mary Donnelly
T.D. Raymond--Don Burroughs
John McFarlan--Henry Hull
Reviews: R139, R141, R144, R145, R147, R148, R149, R156, R165, R166, R167, R169.

P16 *MARY THE THIRD*

P16.1 *Mary the Third* opened 5 February 1923 at the 39th Street Theatre. Produced by Lee Shubert in association with Mary Kirkpatrick. 160 performances. It was chosen one of the best plays of 1923 by Burns Mantle.
Mary the First, 1870--Louise Huff
William--Ben Lyon

Mary the Second, 1897--Louise Huff
Robert--Ben Lyon
Richard--William Hanley

Mary the Third, 1923--Louise Huff
Mother--Beatrice Terry
Granny--May Galyer
Father--George Howard
Bobby--Morgan Farley
Lynn--Ben Lyon
Hal--William Hanley

Lettie--Mildred McCleod
Max--John A. Kirkpatrick
Nora--Elinor Montell
Reviews: R171, R172, R173, R175, R176, R177, R178, R179, R180, R181, R183, R184.

P17 *EXPRESSING WILLIE*

P17.1 *Expressing Willie* opened 16 April 1924 at the 48th Street Theatre. Produced by the Equity players, staged and directed by Crothers. 281 performances.
Minnie Whitcomb--Chrystal Herne
Willie Smith--Richard Sterling
Mrs. Smith--Louise Closser Hale
Taliaferro--Alan Brooks
George Cadwalader--Warren William
Dolly Cadwalader--Molly MacIntyre
Frances Sylvester--Merle Maddern
Simpson--Douglas Garden
Reynolds--John Gerard
Jean--Louise Waller
Gordon--James Bell
Reviews:R184, R185, R186, R187, R188, R189, R190.

P18 *A LADY'S VIRTUE*

P18.1 *A Lady's Virtue* opened 23 November 1925 at the Bijou Theatre. Produced by Lee and J.J. Shubert, staged by Crothers. Settings by Watson Barrett. 136 performances.
Mrs. Lucas--Isabel Irving
Sally Halstead--Florence Nash
Madame Sisson--Mary Nash
Walter Lucas--George Barbier
Ralph Lucas--George Meeker
Harry Halstead--Robert Warwick
Eugenio--Guido Nadzo
Tshstanoff--Martin Berkeley
Montie--Joseph King
A Maid--Florence Arlington
Reviews: R191, R192, R193, R194, R195.

P19 *VENUS*

P19.1 *Venus* opened 26 December 1927 at the Masque Theatre. Produced by

Carl Reed, staged by Crothers. Settings by Livingston Platt. 8 performances.
  Virgie Gibbs--Cecilia Loftus
  Mason--Charlie Hampden
  Dr. Dickie Wakely--Arnold Lucy
  Herbert Beveredge--Tyrone Power
  Agnes Beveredge--Patricia Collinge
  Diana Gibbs--Katharine Francis
  Ross Hurst--Edward Crandall
Reviews: R197, R199, R200.

P20 *LET US BE GAY*

P20.1 *Let Us Be Gay* opened 21 February 1929 at the Little Theatre. Produced by John Golden, directed by Crothers. 132 performances. It was chosen one of the Best Plays of 1929 by Burns Mantle.
  Kitty Brown--Francine Larrimore
  Bob Brown--Warren Williams
  Mrs. Boucicault--Charlotte Granville
  Dierdre Lessing--Rita Vale
  Townley Town--Kenneth Hunter
  Bruce Keen--Ross Alexander
  Madge Livingston--Adele Klaer
  Wallace Grainger--Gilbert Douglas
  Whitman--St. Clair Bayfield
  Struthers--George Wright, Jr.
  Williams--James C. Lane
  Perkins--Natalie Potter
Reviews: R201, R202, R203, R204, R205, R206, R207, R208.

P21 *AS HUSBANDS GO*

P21.1 *As Husbands Go* opened 5 March 1931 at the John Golden Theatre. Produced by John Golden, directed by Crothers. 148 performances. It was selected as one of Best Plays of 1931 by Burns Mantle.
  Lucile Lingard--Lily Cahill
  Ronald Derbyshire--Geoffrey Wardwell
  Emmie Sykes--Catharine Doucet
  Hippolitus Lomi--Roman Bohnen
  Maitre D'Hotel--Francois Steyaert
  Waiter--Bruno Wick
  Charles Lingard--Jay Fassett
  Wilbur--Eddie Wragge
  Christine--Mathilde Baring
  Peggy Sykes--Marjorie Lytell
  Jake Canon--Robert Foulk

Katie--Ruth Windsor
Reviews: R212, R213, R215, R217, R219, R226, R228, R229, R230, R231, R232.

P21.2 The play was revived at the Forest Theatre, produced by O.E. Wee and J.J. Leventhal, Inc. and staged by Crothers in January 1933.
Lucile--Alice Frost
Ronald--Leslie Denison
Emmie--Sue Keller
Hippolitus--Ben McQuarrie
Charles--Joseph King
Maitre D'--Arthur Mark
Waiter--Bruno Wick
Wilbur--Norman Williams
Christine--Mathilda Baring
Peggy--Marjorie Lytell
Jake--Robert Foulk
Katie--Margo Fiske
Review: R245.

P22 *CAUGHT WET*

P22.1 *Caught Wet* opened 4 November 1931 at the John Golden Theatre. Produced by John Golden, staged by Crothers. 13 performances.
Clifford Vanderstyle--Michal Milan
Julia Vanderstyle--Dortha Duckworth
Peter Smeed--Bertram Thorn
Tommy Jones--Geoffrey Bryant
Michael Meer--Robert Lowes
Dolores Winthrop--Gertrude Michael
Elizabeth Betts--Sylvia Field
Stanley--Joseph King
Brewster--Allan Hale
Peterson--Robert Bruce
A Watchman--James Davey
Reviews: R221, R222, R224, R239.

P23 *WHEN LADIES MEET*

P23.1 *When Ladies Meet* opened 6 October 1932 at the Royale Theatre. Produced by John Golden, staged by Crothers. A return engagement at the Royale opened 15 May 1933. 173 performances; the return 18 performances. It was selected one of the Best Plays of 1932-33 by Burns Mantle.
Mary Howard--Frieda Inescort
Jimmie Lee--Walter Abel
Mrs. Bridget Drake--Spring Byington

Walter Manners--Robert Lowes
Rogers Woodruff--Herbert Rawlinson
Pierre--Auguste Aramini
Claire Woodruff--Selena Royle
Reviews: R233, R234, R235, R236, R237, R238, R240, R241, R242, R244, R247.

P24 *SUSAN AND GOD*

P24.1 *Susan and God* opened 7 October 1937 at the Plymouth Theatre. Produced by John Golden, staged by Crothers. Settings by Jo Mielziner. 288 performances. Chosen as one of the Best Plays of 1937-38 by Burns Mantle, it also won the Gold Medal of the Theatre Group as outstanding American play of the season. It was revived in December 1943, again with Gertrude Lawrence, at the City Center.

Susan Trexel--Gertrude Lawrence
Barrie Trexel--Paul McGrath
Blossom Trexel--Nancy Kelly
Irene Burroughs--Vera Allen
Michael O'Hara--Frank Fenton
Charlotte Marley--Eleanor Audley
Hutchins Stubbs--Fred Leslie
Leonora Stubbs--Edith Atwater
Clyde Rochester--David Byrne
Leeds--John D. Seymor
Leontine--Katherine Deane
Reviews: R248, R249, R251, R252, R253, R254, R256, R257.

Author Index

This index lists all critics and scholars included in the secondary bibliography. The references are keyed to the numbers assigned to each entry in the bibliography.

General Index

The General Index lists textual references and references keyed to the primary ("A" listings) and secondary ("B," "I" and "R" listings) bibliographies.

About the Authors

COLETTE LINDROTH is Professor of English at Caldwell College. Her articles have appeared in journals such as *Literature/Film Quarterly*.

JAMES LINDROTH is Professor of English at Seton Hall University. His work has been published in *Modern Fiction Studies* and *Religion and Literature*.

Recent Titles in
Modern Dramatists Research and Production Sourcebooks

Clifford Odets: A Research and Production Sourcebook
William W. Demastes

T. S. Eliot's Drama: A Research and Production Sourcebook
Randy Malamud

S. N. Behrman: A Research and Production Sourcebook
Robert F. Gross

Susan Glaspell: A Research and Production Sourcebook
Mary E. Papke

William Inge: A Research and Production Sourcebook
Richard M. Leeson

William Saroyan: A Research and Production Sourcebook
Jon Whitmore

Clare Boothe Luce: A Research and Production Sourcebook
Mark Fearnow

www.ingramcontent.com/pod-product-compliance
Lightning Source LLC
Chambersburg PA
CBHW070442100426
42812CB00004B/1187